A New Commandment
Toward a Renewed Rite for the Washing of Feet

Peter Jeffery

A Liturgical Press Book

THE LITURGICAL PRESS
Collegeville, Minnesota

Cover design by Richard L. Haeg

1   2   3   4   5   6   7   8   9

Library of Congress Cataloging-in-Publication Data

Jeffery, Peter, 1953–
    A new commandment : toward a renewed rite for the washing of feet / Peter Jeffery.
        p.   cm.
    Includes bibliographical references.
    ISBN 0-8146-2004-3
    1. Foot washing (Rite)—History of doctrines—Catholic Church.
    2. Maundy Thursday—History of doctrines—Catholic Church.
    3. Catholic Church—Liturgy.   I. Title.
    BV8733.F7J44   1992
    264′02099—dc20   92-17174
                                                      CIP

Contents

I. The Present Rite of Footwashing:
Some Pastoral Difficulties 5

II. The Footwashing in the Gospel 13

III. Liturgical Traditions of Washing Feet 15

   A. Footwashings in Christian Initiation 15
   B. Monastic Footwashings 18
   C. Survivals of Footwashing Among the Laity 21
   D. Footwashing Traditions for Holy Thursday 25
      1. Ceremonies Derived from the
         Mandatum Fratrum 26
      2. A Ceremony Derived from the
         Mandatum Pauperum 29

IV. The Meaning of the Footwashing 33

   A. What the Liturgical Texts Say 33
   B. The Participation of Women in Footwashings 39

V. The Reform of 1956 45

   A. Principles Underlying the Reform 45
   B. Issues Raised by the Reform 50
      1. Footwashing and Modern Culture 50
      2. Service to the Poor 51
      3. Liturgical Drama 52

VI. The Footwashing Since Vatican II 59

VII. Toward a Renewed Rite for the Washing of Feet 64

    A. Introduction 64
    B. The Mandatum: A Proposed Rite for
       the Washing of Feet 66

       1. The Meaning of the Footwashing Rite 66
       2. Those Whose Feet May Be Washed 67
       3. Those Who Wash the Feet 68
       4. Environments and Contexts
          for Footwashing Ceremonies 68
       5 . The Order of Service 69

VIII. Conclusion 79

I

The Present Rite of Footwashing: Some Pastoral Difficulties

In recent years, the Roman Catholic Church in the United States has witnessed a controversy over the rite of footwashing celebrated on Holy Thursday, traditionally known as the *Mandatum* ("Commandment"). A few bishops (the number has always been small) have attempted to prevent women from being included among those whose feet are washed, even though this has been widely practiced since at least the 1970s. The exclusion of women has been justified by appeal to the original Latin rubrics of the Sacramentary, which describes the participants as "males" *(viri)*. Thus, it is argued, only the feet of males may be washed during this service.[1] However, at least one Eastern rite diocese has adopted a similar

---

[1]*Missale Romanum ex Decreto Sacrosancti Œcumenici Concilii Vaticani II Instauratum, Auctoritate Pauli Pp. VI Promulgatum,* editio typica altera (Vatican City: Typis Polyglottis Vaticanis, 1975) 244. In the official English translation the word is rendered as "men," which word of course has a history of being used to refer to humans in general. See, for instance, *The Sacramentary Approved for Use in the Dioceses of the United States of America by the National Conference of Catholic Bishops and Confirmed by the Apostolic See: English Translation Prepared by the International Committee on English in the Liturgy* (Collegeville, Minnesota: The Liturgical Press, 1985) 208.

policy in its liturgical regulations, even though it does not use the Roman Sacramentary.[2]

Media reports show that, in the affected dioceses, the price of this adherence to the literal Latin text has been high. As one pastor told a newspaper reporter, "All of a sudden, Holy Thursday becomes an issue of separating into sides."[3] In some places people organized unofficial alternative footwashings, or even handwashings, complying literally with the command not to wash women's feet in order to emphasize their non-compliance with (what they believed to be) its sexist spirit. Some pastors omitted the footwashing altogether rather than face the negative reaction that might have resulted (the Sacramentary permits this omission, "depending on pastoral circumstances").

It is, of course, the duty of bishops to ensure the correct celebration of the liturgy, and there are times when the Church leadership must uphold important principles even though they are currently unpopular. But is this one of those times? What indeed are the underlying principles that determine who should take part in the footwashing? What dogmas of faith or morals would be threatened if women were to be included? What exactly are those who would exclude women defending, and against whom are they defending it? Are these principles so important that it is worth the great pastoral price that is be-

---

[2]In 1989 the Diocese of St. Maron, which represents the Maronite rite in the United States, reformed its liturgical regulations. According to a summary published in the diocesan newspaper, the directives for Thursday of the Mysteries (Holy Thursday) state that "for the Rite of 'The Washing of the Feet,' only men or boys are to be washed (not women or girls)." See "Letter from Msgr. Joseph Joseph," *The Challenge: Diocese of St. Maron—U.S.A.* vol. 12, no. 4 (February 25, 1990) 5. The basis for this regulation is not stated however, for the Maronite rite does not use the current Roman Sacramentary. Nothing is said about the gender of those who are washed in *The Maronite Liturgical Year* 2: *Season of the Great Lent, Passion Week* (n.p.: Diocese of St. Maron—U.S.A., 1982) 143-44.

[3]Quoted in the story "Foot flap flares over Holy Thursday rite," *National Catholic Reporter* vol. 25, no. 18 (February 24, 1989) p. 6, col. 4.

ing paid to uphold them? These questions have been given conflicting answers.

One of the bishops involved, writing in his diocesan paper, offered the explanation that the footwashing ceremony "is the celebration of the institution of the priesthood, where Christ washed the feet of the apostles—all men." [4] But this explanation seems to contradict several aspects of the renewed post-Conciliar liturgy. If it is the footwashing that commemorates the institution of the priesthood at the Last Supper, why did the reform of the Sacramentary after Vatican II introduce a Renewal of Commitment to Priestly Service into the Chrism Mass, which is celebrated in cathedrals on Holy Thursday morning? [5] If the washing of male feet commemorates the ordination of the apostles into the priesthood, why have modern reforms opened the ceremony to include laymen? Would it not be better to wash only the feet of the clergy, as directed in the ("Tridentine") Missal of Pius V?

Asked for its opinion, the Bishops' Committee on the Liturgy issued a statement that favored the inclusion of women. Basing itself on a completely different (and of course better informed) interpretation of the footwashing ceremony, the Committee wrote:

> The principal and traditional meaning of the Holy Thursday *mandatum* . . . is the biblical injunction of Christian charity: Christ's disciples are to love one another.
>
> Because the Gospel of the *mandatum* read on Holy Thursday also depicts Jesus as the "Teacher and Lord" who humbly serves his disciples by performing this extraordinary gesture which goes beyond the laws of hospitality, the element of humble service has accentuated the celebration of the foot-

[4] Quoted in "Priests protest foot-washing stance," *National Catholic Reporter* vol. 25, no. 22 (March 24, 1989) p. 3, col. 4.

[5] The text makes clear that it is this ceremony that commemorates the institution of the priesthood: "Today we celebrate the memory of the first eucharist, at which our Lord Jesus Christ shared with his apostles and with us his call to the priestly service of his Church." *The Sacramentary,* 204.

washing rite in the United States over the last decade or more. In this regard it has become customary in many places to invite both men and women to be participants in this rite in recognition of the service that should be given by all the faithful to the church and to the world. Thus, in the United States, a variation in the rite developed in which not only charity is signified but also humble service.

While this variation may differ from the rubric of the Sacramentary, which mentions only men *("viri selecti"),* it may nevertheless be said that the intention to emphasize service along with charity in the celebration of the rite is an understandable way of accentuating the evangelical command of the Lord, "who came to serve and not to be served," that all members of the church must serve one another in love.

The liturgy is always an act of ecclesial unity and Christian charity, of which the Holy Thursday footwashing rite is an eminent sign. All should obey the Lord's new commandment to love one another *with an abundance of love,* especially at this most sacred time of the liturgical year when the Lord's passion, death and resurrection are remembered and celebrated in the powerful rites of the Triduum.[6]

This document raises questions too. It seems to say that the inclusion of women in the ceremony is something new, justified (only?) by a secondary interpretation that has arisen recently in America ("the element of humble service") alongside "the principal and traditional" interpretation ("Christian charity"). Surely the BCL did not mean to say that women are not included in Christian charity, but only in humble service. Further, by calling the American practice of including women a "variation," it seems to assume that the use of the word "viri" in the Sacramentary represents the traditional practice of the Church. It is hardly surprising, then, that some cautious souls have hesitated to accept this new de-

[6]"Women and the Holy Thursday Foot-Washing Ceremony," issued by the Secretariat of the Bishops' Committee on the Liturgy, February 16, 1987. The full text was published in *Origins: National Catholic Documentary Service* vol. 16, no. 40 (March 19, 1987) 712. The italics are original.

velopment, wondering if it is indeed a legitimate one, and doubting that the Committee's statement could be regarded as definitive. Episcopal directives banning women have thus continued to be issued—indeed they have become an annual Lenten event. Other bishops, while avoiding public statements, seem to have chosen the safer course by quietly using only males in their own celebrations. At least one parish is rumored to have declined a visit from its bishop rather than comply with his private request that only males be brought up for the footwashing. The final authoritative decision that has been sought from Rome is still awaited.[7]

Many in the Church and in the media suspect that the real motivation for the exclusion of women is simple misogyny, perhaps (and no less disturbingly) combined with a lust for power so absolute that it can compel obedience to the very letter of official Latin texts, even when the historical or theological reasons for the wording are unclear, and even when the pastoral consequences are very negative. There are even those who suspect that the affair is really a proxy skirmish over the more important issue of whether women should be admitted to priestly ordination. Given the traditional American concern for fairness, to say nothing of our instinctive distrust of authority figures, these suspicions are unlikely to disappear on their own. Nor will they be overcome by further assertions of ecclesiastical authority, or by appeals to alleged ancient tradition. Like so many other impasses in Church history, this one will only be made passable again through critical study of the historical and theological sources bearing on the problem. Anyone familiar with the recent his-

[7]According to the preamble to the BCL statement, "The matter is being referred to the competent Roman congregation." Ibid. The letter *Paschalis sollemnitatis,* issued by the Congregation for Divine Worship in 1988, "adds no further comments on the exclusion of women, . . . [though] the document's subdued treatment of this issue suggests that the rite and its meaning are considered paramount, not the sex of those whose feet are washed." See John M. Huels, "Chronicle: Preparing and Celebrating the Paschal Feasts," *Worship* 63 (1989) 71–79, especially 77.

tory of the liturgical and ecumenical movements knows that
some of the most intractable issues dividing different groups
of Christians are being remarkably transformed into areas of
increasing convergence, as new historical and theological
scholarship has made it possible to see each problem in a new
context and a different light. The same could happen with
the footwashing issue if, in a spirit of scholarly objectivity,
we would only ask again what the ceremony has meant in
the history of the liturgy, how this meaning has been expressed
in the liturgies of the past, and how it might best be expressed
today. Fortunately there have been some important scholarly
monographs on the history of the footwashing.[8] Consulting
them, we can determine fairly quickly that both sides in the
present stalemate are working from erroneous presuppositions,
and ignoring relevant historical facts. The facts are that women
were never officially excluded from the footwashing ceremony
before the mid-twentieth century—indeed under some circumstances they participated in it fully, both as washers and as
washed. The word "viri," limiting the rite to males, never
appeared in the Roman Missal or in any other liturgical source
prior to the reform of Holy Week in 1956. Its introduction
at that time was part of a knowing and deliberate (though
of course well-intentioned) attempt to replace the traditional
ceremony with something quite different, markedly depart-
ing from both recent practice and the more distant past. The
decision to make this change was never subjected to sufficient
theological or scholarly debate, but now that it has resulted

---

[8]Thomas Schäfer, O.S.B., *Die Fusswaschung im monastische Brauchtum und
in der lateinischen Liturgie: Liturgiegeschichtliche Untersuchung,* Texte und Ar-
beiten, I. Abteilung, Heft 47 (Beuron: Beuroner Kunstverlag, 1956). Pier
Franco Beatrice, *La lavanda dei piedi: Contributo alla storia delle antiche liturgie
cristiane,* Bibliotheca "Ephemerides Liturgicae," "Subsidia" 28 (Rome:
Edizioni Liturgiche, 1983). Schäfer's book, as the title promises, focuses
almost exclusively on Western and monastic developments. Beatrice's book
attempts to treat Eastern and Western evidence equally, but is largely limited to the patristic period. Thus there is still room for further study of
the later medieval and post-medieval practices in both East and West.

in a serious pastoral problem, its reconsideration is long overdue. In my opinion, such a reconsideration will lead inex-
orably to the conviction that the entire footwashing rite, as
presently found in the Sacramentary, is fundamentally flawed,
and must be replaced as soon as possible with a rite that returns
to the authentic liturgical tradition. Such a rite, by its very
nature, would make it impossible even to question the legiti-
macy of full participation by women, for about this the historical sources permit no doubt. The purpose of the present book
is to demonstrate briefly that these things are so, with a few
carefully chosen historical examples.

II

The Footwashing in the Gospel

The story of how Jesus washed the feet of his disciples at the Last Supper is told only in the Gospel of John (13:2-20).[9] According to the eminent authority Raymond Brown, the evangelist himself offered two different interpretations of Jesus' action. The first interpretation is conveyed by the dialogue between Jesus and Peter (13:6-11). After Peter objected, "You shall not wash my feet—ever!" Jesus replied, "If I do not wash you, you will have no heritage with me." Peter immediately responded "Lord, then not only my feet, but my hands and face as well." Jesus answered, "The one who has bathed has no need to wash [except for his feet]; he is clean all over." "Therefore," writes Brown, "it is clear that the footwashing is something that makes it possible for the disciples to have eternal life with Jesus. Such emphasis is intelligible if we understand the footwashing as a symbol for Jesus' salvific death. . . . Jesus performed this servile task to prophesy symbolically that he was about to be humiliated in death. Peter's questioning, provoked by the action, enables Jesus to explain

---

[9]Frédéric Manns has explored some possible Jewish backgrounds for Jesus' action in "Le lavement des pieds: Essai sur la structure et la signification de Jean 13," *Revue des Sciences religieuses* 55 (1981) 149-69.

the salvific necessity of his death: it would bring men their heritage with him and it would cleanse them of sin.''[10]

"The second interpretation of the footwashing is that Jesus has acted out for his disciples an example which they must be prepared to imitate," an example of loving service to others. This is expressed in Jesus' monologue (13:12-20):

> Do you understand what I have done for you?
> You address me as 'Teacher' and 'Lord,'
> and rightly so, for that is what I am.
> Now, if I washed your feet,
> even though I am Lord and Teacher,
> you too must wash one another's feet.
> For it was an example that I gave you:
> you are to do exactly as I have done for you.

"Even taken simply as an example of humility, the footwashing does not lose its association with the death of Jesus; the general context would indicate this. Therefore [John] xv 12-13, with its command to carry love to the point of laying down one's life for others, is an excellent commentary on what Jesus means in xiii 15 when he says: 'You are to do exactly as I have done for you.' ''[11]

[10]Raymond E. Brown, S.S., *The Gospel According to John (xiii–xxi),* The Anchor Bible, vol. 29A (Garden City, N.Y.: Doubleday, 1970) 548, 566, 568.

[11]Brown, *John,* 548-49, 569.

III

Liturgical Traditions
of Washing Feet

Those who feel that modern Biblical criticism has too often discarded the traditional interpretations of cherished scriptural passages will be relieved to learn that has not happened here: Both the interpretations detected by Brown in the gospel text were also expressed in the earliest liturgical tradition. Participation in the death of Jesus was signified by footwashing ceremonies that were included among the rites of Christian initiation. Jesus' example of service was expressed by rites in which Christians washed each other's feet, as well as the feet of poor people and guests. It was the latter practice that developed into the footwashing of Holy Thursday.

A. Footwashings in Christian Initiation

The initiatory footwashing was never a universal practice, and ancient writers disagreed about it.[12] Best known today

[12]In a letter to a certain Januarius written about the year 400, St. Augustine reported that there were a variety of views and practices relative to the footwashing: "Concerning the washing of feet, although the Lord commended it as a form of the humility which He had come to teach, as He later explained, the question is raised about the time when such a great

15

are the remarks of St. Ambrose of Milan, whose sermons "On the Mysteries" and "On the Sacraments" were delivered in the late fourth century, to explain the rites of initiation to the newly baptized. Ambrose clearly accepted both interpretations, but he valued the "mystery and sanctification" of baptism into Jesus' death much more than the example of humility that some of his contemporaries (including his own disciple St. Augustine of Hippo) preferred. This passage has attracted much attention in modern times because of what it says about the liturgical leadership of Rome. In reading it, one should remember that the Greek word "mystery" was something of a synonym for "sacrament," and that in Ambrose's time neither the definitive numbering of the seven sacraments, nor the concomitant distinction between "sacrament" and "sacramental," had been fully worked out.

> You came up out of the font. What then? You listened to the reading. The high priest put on an apron. . . . What does this mystery mean? You must have heard it read that when the Lord had washed the feet of the other disciples he came to Peter, and Peter said to him: "Do you wash my feet?" . . . See all the righteousness, see the humility, see the grace, see the holiness. "If I do not wash your feet," [Jesus] said, "you have no part in me."

practice should best be taught by example, and it coincided with that time at which His teaching made a deeper religious appeal [i.e., Easter]. Many have been unwilling to accept it as a custom, lest it should seen to be a part of the sacrament of baptism. Some have not even shrunk from abolishing it as a custom. But others, in order to promote it at a less conspicuous time, and to separate it from the sacrament of baptism, have chosen to do it either on the third day of the octave [of Easter]—because the number three has such pre-eminence in many sacraments—or on the octave day itself." *Saint Augustine, Letters 1 (1–82),* trans. Sister Wilfrid Parsons, The Fathers of the Church: A New Translation 12 (New York: Fathers of the Church, 1951) 289. For the Latin text see *S. Aurelii Augustini Hipponiensis Episcopi Epistulae,* ed. Al. Goldbacher, Corpus Scriptorum Ecclesiasticorum Latinorum 34/2 (Vienna: F. Tempsky, 1898) 207–08. For further comment see Beatrice, *Lavanda,* 131–33.

We are aware that the Roman Church does not follow this custom, although we take her as our prototype, and follow her rite in everything. But she does not have this rite of the washing of the feet. Perhaps it is because of the large numbers that she has ceased to practice it. But there are those who try to excuse themselves by saying that it should not be performed as a mystery, not as part of the baptismal rite, not for regeneration, but that this washing of the feet should be done as a host would do it for his guests. However, humility is one thing, sanctification another. You must know that this washing is a mystery and sanctification. ''If I do not wash your feet, you shall have no part with me.'' I am not saying this as censuring others; I am simply recommending our own rite. I wish to follow the Roman Church in everything: but we too are not devoid of common sense. When a better custom is kept elsewhere, we are right to keep it here also.

We follow the apostle Peter himself . . . , and he was the priest of the Roman Church. . . . Consider his faith. When he refused at first, this was because of his humility. The submission he made afterwards came from devotion and faith.[13]

In other words, Peter immediately recognized Jesus' example of humility, but his dialogue with Jesus brought him to a deeper recognition, through ''devotion and faith,'' that ''this washing is a mystery and sanctification,'' an opportunity to share a part or heritage with Jesus who would soon die and rise again. Ambrose's words give no indication that the footwashing was restricted to males, and as an essential part of the baptismal rite at Milan, it is hard to see how it could have been. Like the saving death of Jesus itself, this rite was doubtless available to everyone.

In time Ambrose's opponents seem to have won out, and the washing of feet disappeared from baptismal services. A vestige of it survived, however, in the interpretation of Jesus'

---

[13]*De Sacramentis* III, 4–6. The translation is that of Edward Yarnold, S.J., *The Awe-Inspiring Rites of Initiation: Baptismal Homilies of the Fourth Century* (Middlegreen, England: St. Paul Publications, 1972) 122–23.

words "The one who has bathed has no need to wash [except for his feet]" as a reference to sacramental absolution, a kind of "re-washing" for sins committed after baptism. This interpretation, which stems from the exegesis of St. Augustine, has less support from modern biblical criticism, but it influenced Western Christians to see footwashings as acts of penance.[14]

B. Monastic Footwashings

As the baptismal footwashing fell into disuse, it left the field to the other type of footwashing, which emphasized Jesus' humble example. This type must already have existed in New Testament times, when a woman could not be enrolled as a widow unless she had "been hospitable to strangers and washed the feet of God's holy people" (1 Timothy 5:10). This text already exhibits the twofold directionality that would characterize the entire history of the footwashing, connecting it on the one hand with hospitality towards strangers, pilgrims, and guests, and on the other hand with humble service toward fellow Christians. These two emphases remained central to the history of the rite, and eventually led to the development of two different kinds of footwashing services. And just as the quote from 1 Timothy envisions the footwashing as a special ministry of consecrated widows, so the two types of footwashing that eventually developed were practiced especially in religious and monastic communities.

For the Western monastic practice, the key source of information is of course the sixth-century Benedictine Rule, which indeed played a crucial role in the historical development of the footwashing services. Of course the practice was by no means restricted to Benedictines—St. Benedict himself was transmitting and synthesizing longstanding earlier practices inherited, both directly and indirectly, from many Eastern and Western sources.

[14]Beatrice, *Lavanda,* 145-50. Brown, *John,* 567-68.

The Rule gives much importance to the treatment of guests, including guests who are not Christians. Visitors are seen as providing an important opportunity to practice the humble, loving service that Jesus requires of all his followers:

> All guests who present themselves are to be welcomed as Christ, for he himself will say: "I was a stranger and you welcomed me" [Matthew 25:35]. Proper honor must be shown "to all, especially to those who share our faith" [Galatians 6:10] and to pilgrims.
>
> Once a guest has been announced, the superior and the brothers are to meet him with all the courtesy of love. . . . By a bow of the head or by a complete prostration of the body, Christ is to be adored because he is indeed welcomed in them. . . . The divine law is read to the guest for his instruction, and after that every kindness is shown to him. . . . The abbot shall pour water on the hands of the guests, and the abbot with the entire community shall wash their feet. After the washing they will recite this verse: "God, we have received your mercy in the midst of your temple" [Psalm 48:10].
>
> Great care and concern are to be shown in receiving poor people and pilgrims, because in them more particularly Christ is received; our very awe of the rich guarantees them special respect.[15]

Within the community there was also a weekly footwashing, and it too was an opportunity for loving service.

> The brothers should serve one another. Consequently, no one will be excused from kitchen service unless he is sick or engaged in some important business of the monastery, for such service increases reward and fosters love. . . . Let all the rest serve one another in love.
>
> On Saturday the brother who is completing his work will do the washing. He is to wash the towels which the brothers use to wipe their hands and feet. Both the one who is ending

[15]53:1-15. The translation is that of *RB 1980: The Rule of St. Benedict in Latin and English with Notes,* ed. Timothy Fry, O.S.B., et al. (Collegeville, Minnesota: The Liturgical Press, 1981) 255–59.

his service and the one who is about to begin are to wash the
feet of everyone.[16]

The two passages thus reflect the two historical emphases—
towards strangers and guests on the one hand, and towards
fellow Christians (in this case other monks) on the other. These
two traditions became the basis for a long series of historical
developments leading up to the present Holy Thursday rite.
Only the major outlines of this history need to be summarized here.[17]

By the ninth century in the West, the washing of the feet
of guests was often abbreviated to include only those "poor
people and pilgrims" to whom the Benedictine Rule would
accord special honor. It soon became less of a spontaneous
humble service and more of a regular ritual, the *Mandatum
Pauperum.* In some places only a symbolic number of the poor
were actually washed, often as low as three, though at the Ab-
bey of St. Martin of Tours in Marmoutier it was as high as
300.[18] Other common numbers were twelve (recalling the
number of the apostles whose feet Jesus washed) or thirteen
(the significance of which will be explained below). In some
places the number of paupers was determined by the number of monks, for each monk washed the feet of one poor person. The frequency of the washing also varied. In some places
it was done daily throughout the year, in others only weekly,
or only during certain seasons. The washing was most often
celebrated in the evening, but in some places it was done earlier in the day. It frequently included a free meal and dona-
tions of clothing and money to the poor who were involved.

The weekly washing of feet within the community also became more ritualized, the *Mandatum Fratrum.* Schäfer detected
two streams of tradition among Benedictines: In the tradi-

[16]35:1-9. The translation is that of *RB 1980,* 233.

[17]Unless otherwise indicated, the information that follows is taken from
Schäfer, *Fusswaschung.*

[18]Schäfer, *Fusswaschung,* p. 48, n. 111.

tion connected with Benedict of Aniane the footwashing was celebrated before Compline, originally in silence, though in time it came to be accompanied by chants, and to include a handwashing as well. As this tradition developed at Cluny each monk was also given a drink of wine (known as the "Caritas"), a symbol of community joy and perhaps a reminder of the early Christian Agape meal.[19] In the second stream of tradition, associated with Montecassino and Subiaco, the footwashing was a separate service, celebrated in the chapter house after the last meal of the day and closed with a prayer.[20] Among the canons regular, the *Mandatum Fratrum* was seen more as a penitential practice to be done during Lent, but omitted between Easter and Pentecost and on important feasts. The washing was done by the priest, deacon, and subdeacon of the week, for the kitchen was usually staffed by lay people who were not members of the community.[21] In all traditions it was usual for all the members of the community to have their feet washed, not merely a symbolic number. As the Vallumbrosan Benedictine customary directs,

> After the meal, when the clapper has sounded and the brothers have gathered, let the abbot wash and dry the feet of all, even the children. After this let the hebdomadary of the week wash the feet of the abbot, and the hebdomadary of the coming week dry [them].[22]

C. Survivals of the Footwashing Among the Laity

It was perhaps in St. Benedict's time that the washing of feet began to die out among the laity. His approximate contemporary St. Caesarius of Arles, who championed more than

[19]Schäfer, *Fusswaschung,* 63–66.
[20]Schäfer, *Fusswaschung,* 66–68.
[21]Schäfer, *Fusswaschung,* 68–70.
[22]Kassius Hallinger, O.S.B., ed., *Consuetudines Cluniacensium Antiquiores cum redactionibus derivatis,* Corpus Consuetudinum Monasticarum, Tomi VII pars altera (Siegburg: F. Schmitt, 1983) 350–51.

one lost cause, seems to have been swimming against the tide
when he preached this sermon one Holy Thursday:

> Today, dearest brethren, we are going to hear the Evangelist
> say that "when the Lord had risen from the meal, he took
> off his cloak, tied a towel around himself, and began to wash
> his disciples' feet." What shall we say about this occasion,
> most beloved? Or what excuse will we be able to offer, we
> who scorn to give to strangers the service which He deigned
> to offer to His servants? Possibly there are some powerful and
> noble men or delicate women who scorn to bend down to the
> footsteps of the saints who are sojourning [peregrinantium]
> in this world. Not only do they themselves refuse to wash the
> feet of strangers, but neither do they command any of their
> servants to do it for them. Perhaps Christian men or women
> blush to touch the feet of saints and strangers in this world,
> but if they do not amend their lives, they will have more to
> be ashamed of and to lament when they will have to be sepa-
> rated from companionship with them in the future life. Then
> they will be tormented without any remedy of repentance,
> when they shall see those whom they despised receive the king-
> dom because of their humility, while they on account of their
> pride have merited punishment. Let us fear, brethren, what
> the blessed Apostle Peter feared, when he heard the Lord say:
> "If I do not wash you, you will have no share in my heri-
> tage."[23]

In spite of everything, a few vestiges of lay footwashing
managed to survive even into modern times, for the late medieval liturgy occasionally permitted to kings and other high-
ranking laypeople a greater degree of participation than was
available to the rest of the laity. Thus some Christian monarchs
have continued to celebrate the *Mandatum Pauperum* on Holy

[23]Sermo 202, Latin text in Corpus Christianorum, Series Latina 104,
p. 814. This translation is from Saint Caesarius of Arles, *Sermons, vol. III
(187-238)*, trans. Sister Mary Magdeleine Mueller O.S.F., *The Fathers of
the Church* (Washington, D.C.: Catholic University of America Press, 1973)
65. For comment see Beatrice, *Lavanda,* 169.

Thursday, even into the twentieth century.[24] In England, for instance, the king washed one pauper for each year of his age, and also gave each one a free meal and a gift of money. Thus as he drew nearer in age to the biblical "threescore years and ten" (Psalm 90:10), and as the number of paupers to be washed and fed increased annually, the more ruefully he may have recalled the saying "The poor you have always with you" (John 12:8). The English tradition even survived the Reformation; Queen Elizabeth I (1533–1603) is said to have washed annually the feet of poor women with perfumed water from a silver bowl, even though the Church of England had no rite of footwashing in the Book of Common Prayer. By the early twentieth century both the washing and the meal were long forgotten, but every Holy Thursday royal officials still distributed silver coins to the poor, one for each year of the monarch's age.[25]

Where it did not continue as a royal ceremony, the practice of washing feet in the public liturgy generally did not survive among most churches of the Reformation, though the significance of Jesus' action itself was widely recognized, and even played a role in Catholic/Protestant polemic.[26] Doubt-

[24]Francis X. Weiser, *Handbook of Christian Feasts and Customs: The Year of the Lord in Liturgy and Folklore* (New York: Harcourt Brace, 1958) 195–96, 208.

[25]See the article "Maundy Thursday," in *Encyclopedia Britannica*, 11th ed., vol. 17 (Cambridge: Cambridge University Press, 1911) 904–05.

[26]For instance, in Martin Luther's *Passional Christi und Anti-Christi* of 1521, with woodcuts by Lucas Cranach the Elder, a picture of Jesus washing and kissing the feet of Peter is contrasted with a scene of contemporary royalty lining up to kiss the feet of the pope. See *D. Martin Luthers Werke: Kritische Gesamtausgabe* 9 (Weimar: Hermann Böhlau, 1893) 703, and woodcuts 5–6 in the appendix. Interestingly, the gospel text does not state that Jesus kissed the disciples' feet—the impression that he did so came from the liturgical footwashing rite of the period, where this was done. The origin of this practice may be related to the great number of other kisses that were called for in the medieval liturgy when there was physical contact between people of differing status. Thus at High Mass, even into the twentieth century, it was the rule that "Whenever [the deacon] hands anything

less many Protestants would agree with Archbishop of Canterbury Arthur Michael Ramsey, who, in a sermon delivered in the Roman Catholic cathedral in Milwaukee, said that, even though Jesus' action "contains within itself . . . the real essence of Christianity," it is more important to imitate the spirit of this event than to re-enact it liturgically.

> Many times that example of Jesus has been literally followed. Why, in monasteries all over the world on Maundy Thursday night the abbot will wash the feet of the monks in literal imitation of what our Lord did. It is so in seminaries in many places of the world, the foot-washing on that night of the year. And I believe into the last century there were some courts in Europe where a monarch used to wash the feet of his courtiers. But the example that our Lord set is to be followed after the spirit and not just after the letter. And that means that every generation of Christians, seeking the guidance of the Holy Spirit, will be asking, "How can we in our own time be copying this supreme example of our Master?" And today it is perhaps urgent that not only individuals but whole nations should take seriously Christ's example of the service of one another at a time when parts of the world are pretty prosperous and in other parts of the world there is acute poverty and hunger. And every Christian congregation should be earnestly asking itself, "How are we as a Christian congregation going to copy the Lord's example?" And so, too, it is for every man, woman, and child in this great cathedral tonight to take a look at the Lord washing the feet of the apostles, and to put the urgent question in a new way: "Who is my neighbor?" [Luke 10:29]. And it is St. John, to whom this lovely cathedral is dedicated, who tells us that this is after all the practical test of the credibility of our Christianity, that

to the celebrant he first kisses the thing, then the celebrant's hand. When he takes anything from him, he first kisses the hand, then the thing." Every incensing, for instance, involved eight kisses, "He has to kiss the spoon, the hand, the hand, the spoon; the thurible, the hand, the hand, the thurible." See Adrian Fortescue, *The Ceremonies of the Roman Rite Described,* 5th ed., rev. J. B. O'Connell (London: Burns Oates and Washbourne, 1934) 120, xxiii.

"if a man does not love his brother whom he has seen, how shall he love God whom he has not seen?" [1 John 4:20].[27]

The great exception here is the Free Church tradition, in which the Mennonites, for instance, hold footwashings twice a year in connection with the semi-annual communion service.[28] Similar practices are in use also in some denominations of more recent origin.[29] In these traditions it is common for all the members of the congregation to pair off, men with men and women with women, and take turns washing the other's feet.

D. Footwashing Traditions for Holy Thursday

In medieval monastic and religious communities that practiced footwashings regularly, it was only natural that the Holy Thursday footwashing should be treated as one particularly solemn instance of something that was done all year. Thus the medieval and post-medieval rites for Holy Thursday, despite their many variations, are all clearly derived from the *Mandatum Pauperum,* the *Mandatum Fratrum,* or both. In some houses there were as many as three footwashings that day: one for the poor in the morning, one for the lay brothers after Vespers, and one for the monks after the evening meal.[30] Both

[27]Arthur Michael Ramsey, "He Began to Wash Their Feet," *Nashota Review* 16 (1978) 230–34, especially 230–32.

[28]H. S. Bender, "Footwashing," *The Mennonite Encyclopedia: A Comprehensive Reference Work on the Anabaptist-Mennonite Movement* (Scottdale, Penn.: Mennonite Publishing House; Newton, Kan.: Mennonite Publication Office; Hillsboro, Kan.: Mennonite Brethren Publishing House, 1956) vol. 2, 347–51.

[29]A detailed description of the biannual footwashings practiced in a small group of black churches in Mississippi and Alabama will be found in Joy Driskell Baklanoff, "The Celebration of a Feast: Music, Dance, and Possession Trance in the Black Primitive Baptist Footwashing Ritual," *Ethnomusicology* 31 (1987) 381–94.

[30]Hallinger, *Consuetudines,* 349–51.

the *Mandatum Pauperum* and the *Mandatum Fratrum* survived in the standardized Roman liturgical books issued after the Council of Trent, indeed with some uncertainty as to which one ought to be preferred. Whatever was done in practice, this remained the official state of affairs until the reform of Holy Week in 1956.

1. Ceremonies Derived from Mandatum Fratrum

The footwashing rite in the *Missale Romanum* of Pius V (1570), which was celebrated Holy Thursday evening, is a form of the *Mandatum Fratrum,* celebrated among the clergy of each church. Though contained in the Missal, it had no actual connection to the Mass of the day; thus the gospel story had to be read again, even though it had already been read at Mass earlier in the afternoon.

> After the stripping of the altars, at a convenient hour a signal is given with the clapper, and the clergy meet together for the Maundy. The prelate or superior wears a purple stole and cope over his amice and alb, and at the place appointed puts incense into the thurible, served by the deacon who is in attendance with a subdeacon vested in white, as at mass. Then the deacon, holding the Gospel book before his breast, kneels before the superior and asks a blessing; having received it, while two acolytes stand by with lighted candles and the subdeacon holds the book, he makes the sign of the cross on the book and incenses it and sings, in the usual way, the Gospel [John 13:1-15] . . . as at mass.
>
> After this the subdeacon takes the book open to the superior to kiss, and the deacon incenses him as usual. Then the superior takes off his cope and is girded with a linen towel by the deacon and subdeacon, and so girded, goes to wash the feet; clerks serve a basin and water. While the subdeacon holds the right foot of each of those whose feet are to be washed, the superior, kneeling before him, washes his foot, wipes and kisses it, the deacon handing a towel for the wiping. Meanwhile the following [antiphons] are sung: . . . . After the washing, the superior or he who washed the feet of the others,

washes his hands and wipes them on another towel: then returning to the place whence he came, he puts on the cope, and standing with his head bare says ''Our Father'' silently [followed by certain other prayers].[31]

This rite never mentions the laity, although some medieval antecedents of it specifically state that the footwashing was to begin only ''after all the laity have been thrown out.''[32] The reason is simply that it was not conceived as a parish celebration, but as a private one within the community of clergy serving each individual church. Consistent with this is the fact that the footwashing was typically celebrated, not in the sanctuary or nave of the church, but in some other place: the narthex or entrance area, the sacristy, the chapter room. At Montecassino, the monks went to the refectory and ate a little, then went to the chapter house where the abbot washed their feet, then returned to the refectory to finish their meal. In this way their footwashing, like the one in the gospel, could be said to have taken place ''during supper'' (John 13:2).[33]

In Rome, a special form of the *Mandatum Fratrum* was used by the Pope, who washed the feet of twelve subdeacons (i.e., the lowest rank of full-fledged clergy) during the singing of Vespers.[34] By the fifteenth century the Pope had also adopted

[31]The Latin text can, of course, be found in any edition of the ''Tridentine'' *Missale Romanum.* I have taken this English translation from *The Missal, Compiled by Lawful Authority from the* Missale Romanum, ed. and trans. Adrian Fortescue (London: Burns Oates and Washbourne, 1922) 285–89.

[32]See Schäfer, *Fusswaschung,* 72: "laicis omnibus foris projectis."

[33]Schäfer, *Fusswaschung,* 74–75.

[34]See the texts published in Michel Andrieu, ed., *Le Pontifical romain au moyen-âge* 2, Studi e Testi 87 (Vatican City: Bibliotheca Apostolica Vaticana, 1940) 463–64. Marc Dykmans, S.J., ed. *Le cérémonial papal de la fin du moyen âge à la Renaissance,* Bibliothèque de l'Institut Historique Belge de Rome 24–27 (Brussels and Rome: Insitut Historique Belge de Rome, 1977–1985) vol. 2, 380–81; vol. 3, 210–11; vol. 4, 139–40. An earlier practice called for the Pope to wash the feet of his chamberlains, see Antoine Chavasse, ''A Rome, le jeudi-saint, au VIIᵉ siècle, d'après un vieil ordo,'' *Revue d'Histoire Ecclésiastique* 50 (1955) 21–35, especially 28.

a form of the *Mandatum Pauperum,* using thirteen paupers rather than twelve.[35] The additional pauper seems to have been inspired by legends of Pope Gregory the Great (reigned 590–604) who is said to have customarily shared his own table with the poor; from time to time he would be visited by a mysterious extra guest who would later turn out (depending on the story) to have been either Jesus or an angel.[36]

In the Ambrosian rite, the archbishop of Milan would wash the feet of the priests, the deacons, the Teacher of the Boys and the Chief Reader, afterward sharing a drink with them "pro caritate."[37] In the East, the patriarch of Constantinople washed the feet of three subdeacons, three deacons, three priests, one archbishop and two metropolitans; the Greek patriarch of Jerusalem washed essentially the same group, but with two bishops and only one metropolitan.[38] The idea was obviously to represent the full range of the clergy—all of whom, of course, were the patriarch's subordinates. The rite of footwashing has largely disappeared from the modern Byzantine rite. One scholar reported in 1900 that he could find only three places where the ceremony was still in use, but that in each of them it was attended by the laity in great numbers.

> One would seek in vain in the modern *typika* [i.e. liturgical books] of the Greek church for the least trace of this interest-

---

[35]Marc Dykmans, S.J., ed., *L'Oeuvre de Patrizi Piccolomini ou le cérémonial papal de la première Renaissance* 2, Studi e Testi 294 (Vatican City: Bibliotheca Apostolica Vaticana, 1982) 373–76.

[36]Brief summaries of the legends will be found in F. Homes Dudden, *Gregory the Great: His Place in History and Thought,* vol. 1 (London and New York: Longmans, Green, 1905) 250.

[37]Marco Magistretti, ed., *Beroldus sive Ecclesiae Ambrosianae Mediolanensis Kalendarium et Ordines saec. XII* (Milan: Giovanola, 1894) 105.

[38]For Constantinople, see Juan Mateos, S.J., ed., *Le Typicon de la grande église* 2, Orientalia Christiana Analecta 166 (Rome: Pontificium Institutum Orientalium Studiorum, 1963) 72–73. For Jerusalem, see A. Papadopoulos-Kerameus, ed., *Analekta Ierosolymitikes Stachyologias* 2 (St. Petersburg: Kirschbaum, 1894; repr. Brussels: Culture et Civilisation, 1963) 113.

ing and pious ceremony, just as for several others which are described in official liturgical books but long ago fell into disuse for unknown reasons. Those who confidently accept the audacious affirmations of orthodox polemicists, and still believe in the absolute unchangeability of the Oriental rites, would doubtless be astonished to learn that the washing of feet on Holy Thursday, observed in all important churches and monasteries of the Latin church, is to my knowledge no longer practiced except in three Greek churches. At the monastery of St. John at Patmos, the superior washes the feet of twelve monks each year. A similar ceremony takes place at the monastery of the Forerunner [i.e. St. John the Baptist] at Zindji-Déré, near Caesarea in Cappadocia. There, if one can believe the Greek newspapers of Constantinople, one will see up to 40,000 faithful assisting at the ceremony. Finally, at Jerusalem, the patriarch, bareheaded and with hair unbound, washes on his knees the feet of twelve priests, in the presence of the bishops and other members of the Synod, the clergy and an immense crowd, which covers the terraces and fills the garden opposite the *metochion* of Gethsemane: the ceremony takes place on a platform erected in the court of the church of the Anastasis [i.e. the Holy Sepulchre].[39]

2. A Ceremony Derived from the Mandatum Pauperum

The Roman rite as reformed after the Council of Trent also preserved the tradition of the *Mandatum Pauperum,* in the book for bishops known as the *Caeremoniale Episcoporum* (1600). The text begins by describing a ceremony similar to that of the Missal, but then it runs into confusion over whose feet will be washed.

[39]S. Pétridès, "Le lavement des pieds le jeudi-saint dans l'église grecque," *Échos d'Orient* 3 (1900) 321–26, see p. 323. The ceremony followed at Jerusalem was translated into French in S. Pétridès, "La cérémonie du lavement des pieds à Jérusalem," *Échos d'Orient* 14 (1911) 89–99. Photographs of the ceremony are published in Paschal Kinsel, Leonard Henry, and Alfred Wagg, *The Catholic Shrines of the Holy Land* (New York: Farrar, Straus and Young, 1951) 153–56.

At a convenient hour, the bishop comes to the place prepared for the Mandatum, where he vests in amice, alb, cincture, stole, violet chasuble and simple mitre. But the deacon and the subdeacon who ministered at the Mass assist him in white vestments, in which, except for the maniples, they are to be vested before the bishop comes to the place of the Mandatum. All the canons are to be present, as well as the chaplain with the archiepiscopal cross if the celebrant is an archbishop. There too let the paupers be made ready whose feet are to be washed.

But the rites of the churches are diverse concerning this, for in one place it is the usage to dress thirteen paupers at the Bishop's or Chapter's expense, to refresh them with food and drink, and at the right time to wash their feet and give them alms. Elsewhere bishops wash the feet of thirteen of their canons. Because [of such diversity], this will therefore be left to be done according to the custom of the churches, or the choice of the bishop, who may prefer to do the washing with paupers, even in places where it is the custom to do the washing with canons. For in this way [i.e. by using paupers] it seems to display a greater humility and charity than washing the feet of canons [would do].[40]

---

[40]"Hora competenti Episcopus accedit ad locum praeparatum pro Mandato, ubi induitur amictu, alba, cingulo, stola, pluviali coloris violacei, et mitra simplici. Diaconus autem et Subdiaconus, qui in Missa ministrarunt, eidem assistent cum paramentis albis, quibus praeter manipulos parati erunt antequam Episcopus ad Mandati locum accedat, praesentibus etiam Canonicis, et Capellano cum Cruce archiepiscopali, si Celebrans erit Archiepiscopus, ibique parati sint pauperes, quibus lavandi sunt pedes.

"Sed quia circa hoc diversi sunt ritus ecclesiarum; alicubi enim in usu est, vestire sumptibus Episcopi, vel Capituli tredecim pauperes, eosdemque cibo et potu reficere, et mox suo tempore eisdem pedes lavare, et eleemosynam praebere: alibi Episcopi lavant pedes tredecim ex suis Canonicis; ideo relinquetur hoc faciendum juxta consuetudinem ecclesiarum, vel arbitrio Episcopi, si maluerit pauperibus lavare, etiam in locis, ubi sit consuetudo lavandi Canonicis; videtur enim eo pacto majorem humilitatem, et caritatem praeseferre, quam lavare pedes Canonicis." *Caeremoniale Episcoporum* Liber II, caput xxiv, 1-2. The edition I am using is *Caeremoniale Episcoporum, Clementis VIII., Innocentii X. et Benedicti XIII. Jussu Editum,*

There follows a long description of the rite to be followed if paupers are used, and then a short list of the changes to be made if, instead, the canons are the ones whose feet are washed. How these guidelines were actually put into practice between the sixteenth and the twentieth centuries is a subject that would well repay further research: In a three-way conflict among the powerful forces of local custom, the personal preferences of bishops, and the natural tendency to gravitate towards the Missal as the path of least resistance, what tended to win out? But for our present purposes it is the enunciated principles that matter most.

Benedicti XIV. et Leonis XIII. Auctoritate Recognitum (Turin: P. Marietti, 1924) 184–85.

IV

The Meaning of the Footwashing

A. What the Liturgical Texts Say

The meaning of the footwashing rite is most clearly expressed in the traditional texts of the chants that were sung and the prayers that were said during the ceremony. In the Western Church there were dozens of chants, which were used more or less interchangeably both on Holy Thursday and on other days when there was a Mandatum. Each locality had a somewhat different list,[41] but the series usually began with the antiphon *Mandatum novum do vobis*, " 'A new commandment I give to you, that you love one another as I have loved you,' says the Lord" (John 13:34).[42] It is still found (though moved out of first place) in our modern Sacramentary. It may be this text that gave the name "Mandatum" to the entire

---

[41]For some examples see Manfred F. Bukofzer, *Studies in Medieval and Renaissance Music* (New York: W. W. Norton, 1950) 230–42.

[42]This antiphon and an English rendering of it are given below with Psalm 119:1-8 in the suggested rite of footwashing, p. 70. It is edited from the historic Vatican Edition, now available as *Graduale Sacrosanctae Romanae Ecclesiae* (Solesmes: Abbaye Saint-Pierre, 1974 and subsequent printings) 167. For further information on the latest editions of the Gregorian chant repertory, see Peter Jeffery, "The New Chantbooks from Solesmes," *Notes: The Quarterly Journal of the Music Library Association* 47 (1991) 1039–63.

rite, and even to the day, for the medieval English corruption "Maundy" still survives in the name of Maundy Thursday. The name "Mandatum" or "mandate" also calls attention to the fact that the practice of footwashing was commanded by Jesus, even though it never came to be counted as one of the sacraments he instituted.

Some of the other medieval antiphons quoted or summarized parts of the gospel story, and a few of these remain in our modern Sacramentary. Other antiphon texts, no longer in use, seek to explain the meaning of the ceremony rather than merely recounting what happened at the Last Supper. Here are three that occur in hundreds of sources, from the Romano-Germanic Pontifical of the tenth century[43] to the fifteenth-century Processional of the Benedictine Nuns of Chester, England:[44]

> (1) Let us love one another, because charity is from God. The one who loves his brother is born of God, and lives in him (cf. 1 John 4:7, 16, 21; 5:1).
>
> (2) Where there is charity and love, there is the gathering of the saints. There there is neither anger nor hurt, but steadfast love forever. Christ came down to redeem the world in order to liberate people from death. He gave his disciples an example that they should wash each other's feet.
>
> (3) Christ has brought us together to glorify himself. O Lord, fill our hearts with the Holy Spirit.

[43]Michel Andrieu, ed., *Les Ordines Romani du Haut Moyen Age* 5, Spicilegium Sacrum Lovaniense: Etudes et Documents 29 (Louvain 1961) 228–31. See also Cyrille Vogel and Reinhard Elze, eds., *Le Pontifical romano-germanique du dixième siècle* 2, Studi e Testi 227 (Vatican City: Bibliotheca Apostolica Vaticana, 1963) 77–79.

[44]J. Wickham Legg, ed., *The Processional of the Nuns of Chester,* Henry Bradshaw Society 18 (London: Harrison & Sons, 1899) 9–11, which describes the entire Holy Thursday footwashing (in Middle English). Chants for other footwashings during the year will be found elsewhere in the volume. The medieval manuscript is now in the Huntington Library in San Marino, California, with the number MS EL 34 B7.

English adaptations of two others are given below, with music, in the suggested rite of footwashing.[45]

Of all the medieval chants for the footwashing, the best known today is the hymn *Ubi caritas,* paraphrased in English in the Sacramentary as "Where charity and love are found."[46] But in our Sacramentary it has been moved from the footwashing proper to the offertory procession that follows the footwashing—perhaps a better arrangement than omitting it altogether.

Repeatedly the texts of these chants exhort us to practice humility both in imitation of Jesus and as a means to love and unity among Christians. This theme is also expressed in the hymns of the Eastern Church, although, typically, from a Christological rather than an ecclesiological perspective, emphasizing the mystery of Jesus' divine example more than the Church's response to it:

[45]The antiphon "By this shall they all know" is adapted from *In hoc cognoscent omnes,* as published in the Vatican Edition, *Graduale,* 166–67. The antiphon "The love of Christ" is adapted from *Congregavit nos in unum* in the eleventh-century manuscript Paris, Bibliothèque Nationale, ms f. lat. 903, f. 66v, reproduced *Paléographie musicale* 13 (Solesmes: Abbaye Saint-Pierre, 1925; repr. Bern: Herbert Lang, 1971) 132.

[46]*The Sacramentary,* 209. On the early history of this and similar medieval hymns see the article "Caritas-Lieder" in Bernhard Bischoff, *Mittelalterliche Studien: Ausgewählte Aufsätze zur Schriftkunde und Literaturgeschichte* 2 (Stuttgart: Anton Hiersemann, 1967) 56–77. A Latin text of *Ubi caritas* with a traditional melody is published in *Graduale,* 168. Other Latin texts and English translations set to this melody will be found in *Worship: A Hymnal and Service Book for Roman Catholics,* 3rd ed. (Chicago: GIA Publications, 1986) no. 598 ("Where true love and charity are found"); *The Collegeville Hymnal,* ed. Edward J. McKenna (Collegeville: The Liturgical Press, 1990) nos. 386–87 ("Where charity and love prevail"). The melody is also available with an English text only ("Where true charity and love dwell") in *The Hymnal 1982 according to the use of the Episcopal Church* (New York: Church Hymnal Corporation, 1985) no. 606. English translations set to other melodies have been published in *Worship: A Hymnal* no. 604; *The Hymnal 1982* no. 581; *Lutheran Book of Worship* (Minneapolis: Augsburg Publishing House; Phildelphia: Lutheran Church in America, 1978) no. 126; *The United Methodist Hymnal: Book of United Methodist Worship* (Nashville: The United Methodist Publishing House, 1989) no. 549.

(1) He who made the lakes and springs and seas, wishing to teach us the surpassing value of humility, girded Himself with a towel and washed the feet of the disciples, humbling Himself in the abundance of His great compassion and raising us from the depths of wickedness, for He alone loves mankind.

(2) Humbling Thyself in Thy compassion, Thou hast washed the feet of Thy disciples, teaching them to take the path which as God Thou hast followed. And Peter, who at first refused to be washed, yielded then to the divine command, and earnestly entreated Thee that we may be granted Thy great mercy.

(3) United by the bond of love and offering themselves to Christ the Lord, the apostles were washed clean; and with feet made beautiful, they preached to all the Gospel of peace (cf. Isaiah 52:7).[47]

The second hymn virtually unites the two interpretations of the footwashing. To imitate Jesus' example of humble and compassionate love is indeed to walk the path that he himself trod in the form of a slave—the path leads through death to eternal life, the heritage he shares with those whom he washes.

The penitential interpretation of the footwashing, connecting it with the forgiveness of sins committed after baptism, also made its appearance in medieval chant texts. Indeed, it may understandably have seemed the most obvious interpretation to wealthy and powerful canons who felt humiliated, rather than humbled, by having to wash the feet of wretched beggars.[48] Thus in certain places the *Mandatum Pauperum* was

[47]Mother Mary and Kallistos Ware, trans. *The Lenten Triodion, translated from the original Greek,* The Service Books of the Orthodox Church (London and Boston: Faber and Faber, 1978) 549–51. See also Pétridès, ''La cérémonie.''

[48]A trace of such attitudes can be seen in the unpublished late twelfth-century ordinal of the Augustinian Canons Regular of St. Victor in Paris, wherein the almoner is told to prepare the *Mandatum Pauperum* ''with this considered discretion: let none of them [i.e. the paupers] have cancerous or especially scabrous feet, because of the weak souls of some [canons],

accompanied by the singing of the penitential psalms, or at least Psalm 51 (Latin Psalm 50), which contains the verses "wash me thoroughly from my guilt" and "wash me till I am whiter than snow."[49] Other psalms were also used however, including the three given in the suggested footwashing rite below (Psalms 119, 85, 133), set to melodies adapted from the traditional psalm tones of Gregorian chant.

The penitential interpretation is also expressed in some medieval antiphons that retell the story of the woman who anointed Jesus' feet. Modern exegetes see the several gospel accounts (Matthew 26:6-12, Mark 14:3-9, Luke 7:37-50, and John 12:1-8) as divergent, perhaps based on different original events.[50] But in the Middle Ages they were all assumed to be the same event, and the woman, identified as St. Mary Magdalene, was thought to have been motivated primarily by sorrow for her sins.

The penitential interpretation predominates in the collect *Adesto Domine* that often concluded medieval footwashings and that survived into the *Missale Romanum* of Pius V. It asks "that as outward defilements are here washed away for us and by us, so may the inward sins of us all be washed by you."[51]

so that this sacrament will not be forced or done unwillingly, but rather spontaneously." Paris, Bibliothèque Nationale, ms f. lat. 14506, ff 284v-285. The original Latin reads, "hac considerata discretione: ne quis eorum habeat pedes cancerosos uel nimis scabiosos propter nonnullorum infirmos animos. ut tantum sacramentum non coactum uel non ex animo fiat, sed spontaneum." For more information on this document see Margot Fassler, *Gothic Song: Augustinian Ideals of Reform in the Twelfth Century and the Victorine Sequences* (Cambridge: Cambridge University Press, forthcoming 1992) chs. 6 and 11.

[49]This psalm was also frequently sung in footwashing ceremonies in the Byzantine Rite. See Pétridès, "La cérémonie," 90, 97.

[50]See, for instance, Raymond E. Brown, S.S., *The Gospel According to John I–XII*, The Anchor Bible 29 (Garden City, N.Y.: Doubleday, 1966) 449–54. A more recent discussion is J. F. Coakley, "The Anointing at Bethany and the Priority of John," *Journal of Biblical Literature* 107 (1988) 241–56.

[51]On the origin and history of this collect, see Hermann A. P. Schmidt,

But other collects emphasizing other themes are available, for example in the Romano-Germanic Pontifical of the tenth century,[52] and in Eastern sources.[53] A prayer used by nineteenth-century Benedictines at Beuron, based partly on Gallican models, asks Jesus to "pour out in us those tears which Mary brought forth with much love when she washed your feet." But it also asks for growth in love among the community.[54]

Clearly the main tradition understood the footwashing as explained by the Bishops' Committee on the Liturgy,

S.J., *Hebdomada Sancta 2: Fontes Historici, Commentarius Historicus* (Rome, Freiburg, Barcelona: Herder, 1957) 776. A complete English rendering is given in the proposed ceremony below, p. 76.

[52]Andrieu, *Les Ordines romani* 5, 232; Andrieu, *Le Pontifical romano-germanique* 2, 79. Here is the Latin text of one of them: "Respice, domine, super hos famulos tuos qui se inclinando obedientiae sanctae, pio obsequio fratrum suorum expleverunt servitium, ut semper te habeant in auxilium et in bonis actibus superent inimicum et inoffense semper agant servitium consuetum, ut aeternum a te mereantur percipere premium." An English rendering of this text is given in the suggested renewed rite below, see p. 76.

[53]An English rendering of a prayer used at the footwashing celebrated by the Greek patriarch of Jerusalem is given in the suggested rite, below, pp. 76-77. It is taken from Pétridès, "La cérémonie," 93.

[54]"Deus, totius caritatis confirmator et amator, qui ad hominem humiliatus inclinari dignatus es, ut ad te homo erectus levaretur: annue, quaesumus, familiae tuae in augmento suo exultanti, ita se exercere per dilectionem, ut in te possit unita manere per pacem. Ministra in nobis illas lacrimas, quas Maria, dum tibi pedes abluit, de multa dilectione protulit; fragrare orationem nostram facito, sicut unguentum pisticum sacris plantis infusum Maria fragravit: ut et haec tua domus tota sit in amore et eam pacem consequamur in pectore, quam assecuta est Maria sui osculans Redemptoris vestigia, Salvator mundi: qui vivis et regnas in saecula saeculorum. Amen." Schäfer, *Fusswaschung,* 30-31. Much of the text was adapted from the prayer *Universorum ipse amator,* originally used at the Sign of Peace in the Gallican Mass on Palm Sunday. See Leo Cunibert Mohlberg, ed. *Missale Gothicum (Vat. Reg. lat. 317),* Rerum Ecclesiasticarum Documenta, Series Major: Fontes 5 (Rome: Casa Editrice Herder, 1961) p. 54, no. 199. See also the prayer *Deus totius claritatis* on p. 79, no. 313. A modern adaptation of part of this collect is given below in the suggested rite of footwashing, p. 76.

"Christ's disciples are to love one another." But if this is what the rite ultimately means, it is hard to see why women should be excluded from it. In any case, the historical evidence makes clear that women have taken part throughout the history of the Church.

B. The Participation of Women in Footwashings

The majority of published medieval liturgical sources, like those of the post-Tridentine Roman rite, were intended for use by male religious communities. We have less historical evidence about women for several reasons: their lower rate of literacy meant that fewer of them could write as well as men, and their male contemporaries were less interested in writing about women's lives than about their own. In spite of this there is good evidence that women were as much involved in footwashings as men. Women religious washed the feet of their sisters, and of female paupers and guests, in the same way that men did, using the same rites, prayers and chant texts. Words like "male" and "female" hardly ever occur in the liturgical sources, obviously because gender has nothing to do with the essential meaning of the rite: Jesus' command to follow him in love and humble service is extended to all. The word "viri" in our modern Sacramentary is not a vestige of an ancient or even a recent historical tradition or practice. It was deliberately placed there for the first time, and for dubious reasons, less than forty years ago.

Nevertheless it is probably true that, for most of Christian history, it would have been rare for men and women to participate together in a single footwashing service. Instead religious communities of men and women celebrated separately, each washing the feet of its own members, and those of guests and the poor of the same gender.[55] For most of European history, it would have been so scandalous for women to bare their

[55]For evidence that women religious washed the feet of poor and pilgrim women, see Schäfer, *Fusswaschung,* 41, 50.

feet and legs in public, and have them touched and kissed by celibate males, that there was no need for the authorities to forbid it explicitly. How far the medieval concern for modesty could go is shown by the twelfth-century customary of the Canons Regular of St. Victor in Paris. It instructs the canons to pull their garments tightly around their legs in order to expose no more than their feet, to avoid removing their shoes "inordinately in the presence of the brothers" (they were also forbidden to beat their shoes against the columns, because of noise and the possibility of knocking dirt into each others' eyes). It warns those who dry the feet not to lift up or "immoderately extend" their brothers' shins, not to cross one leg over the other, to wipe only in a downward direction, beginning below the bottom edge of the garment, and to wash their hands immediately afterward.[56] All this was judged necessary even though only male priests would presumably have been present! Clearly the involvement of women in such an undertaking would have been unthinkable. In modern English-speaking North America, on the other hand, people are expected to be more mature; participation by men and women in the same ceremony would provoke far less scandal than the recent attempts to exclude women have done.

But concerns about modesty did not necessarily prevent women from taking an equal part in footwashing ceremonies.

[56]"Fratres extrinsecus intra pratum sedentes inter columnas super marginem pedes suos lauabunt. Vestimenta autem stringent interim manu altera circa crura modeste et pudice, ita ut tamen pedes, et si amplius modicum detecti, appareant. Cum autem lauerint pedes suos, nichilominus pudice siccent eos, tibias in altum non leuantes, nec immoderate extendentes, neque alteram alteri superponentes, sed deorsum positos de sub vestimentis extergant, et calcient, ac deinde eant ad lauatorium et manus lauent. Calceos autem suos uel caligas uel subtalares in praesentia fratrum inordinate non excutiant, neque ad columnas verberent, ut nec strepitum faciant, nec puluerem oculis fratrum iniciant." L. Jocqué and L. Milis, eds. *Liber Ordinis Sancti Victoris Parisiensis,* Corpus Christianorum, Continuatio Medievalis, vol. 61 (Turnhout: Brepols, 1984) 244–45.

The medieval taboos against mixed footwashings were strictly cultural ones, and the separation of the sexes was simply a matter of inculturation, not of the fundamental nature of the rite. Even in those days it was recognized that men and women could wash feet together in extraordinary situations, if all possibility of temptation could somehow be eliminated. One example is this charming tale from a Syriac life of St. Anastasia, who lived in the sixth century:

> The blessed Abba Daniel once left Skete with his disciple to go to a monastery of sisters that was in the inner desert, called Tabennesi. . . .
>
> Toward evening they arrived at the monastery . . . , and the blessed man said to his disciple, "My son, go and tell the abbess 'There is an old man from Skete with me; we would like protection with you tonight.' " Now it was the custom that no man should enter that monastery.
>
> The disciple went off and knocked at the monastery gate. An old nun answered, "Pray, what is it you want?" "Call the abbess for me," he replied. When the abbess came out to him, he told her, "There is an old man from Skete with me, and we would like protection with you tonight, so that we do not get devoured by wild animals." She said to him with a smile, "It would be better for you to be devoured by the wild animals outside, rather than by those inside, my son." He then told her, "The blessed Daniel of Skete is with me."
>
> On hearing this, the abbess did not wait any longer but opened the two gates of the monastery and brought all the sisters out to meet him. From the monastery gate to the place where he was standing, they spread out their veils on the ground, and thus walking over the ground he entered the monastery.
>
> When they had prayed and sat down, the abbess put some water into a basin and washed his feet and those of his disciple. All the sisters then passed in front of him and received a blessing from him. Now the abbess took some of the water that had washed the blessed man's feet and poured some on

the head of each of the sisters as a blessing, while the rest she poured over her own head and into her bosom.[57]

Visitors of blessed Daniel's caliber are rare in any age, and this story may be a pious fiction, recounting an event that never actually took place. Nonetheless it shows that a foot-washing involving both sexes was theoretically conceivable even in those prudish times. If this ceremony were celebrated in a modern American parish, the sight of the abbess washing a man's feet would provoke far fewer comments than the sight of all those nuns putting their veils on the ground for him to walk on.

Women who washed the feet of guests and the poor also practiced the *Mandatum Fratrum.* An important endorsement of this survives in a letter of Pope Zacharias, written in the year 751 to St. Boniface, the "Apostle of Germany" who did so much to promote the spread of the Roman rite to northern Europe.

> For also you have asked this: if it is lawful for religious women, as it is for men, to wash each other's feet, both on Holy Thursday and also on other days. [In fact] this is the Lord's precept, so that whoever fulfills it by faith will have praise from it. For men and women have one Lord, who is in heaven.[58]

It is not clear what motivated Boniface's question, though he was troubled by much that he observed in un-Romanized France and un-Christianized Germany. But there is nothing exceptional about the Pope's reply that Jesus' command was addressed to both men and women. Whenever historical evidence of women's footwashings turns up, they were always

[57]Sebastian P. Brock and Susan Ashbrook Harvey, trans. *Holy Women of the Syrian Orient* (Berkeley and Los Angeles: University of California Press, 1987) 143–44.

[58]Schäfer, *Fusswaschung,* 62. For the complete document see *The Letters of Saint Boniface,* trans. Ephraim Emerton (New York: W. W. Norton, 1976) 159–64, especially 162.

celebrated and understood in the same way as those of the men. A striking example from the Eastern Church comes from the typikon of the monastery of Theotokos Kecharitōmenē ("The Full-of-Grace Mother of God") in Constantinople, founded about the year 1110 by the Empress Irene Doukaina, consort of Alexius Comnenus. It was here that their daughter Anna Comnena, banished for life after failing to overthrow her brother John, wrote the embittered yet fascinating chronicle of Alexius' reign that is now so prized by Byzantine historians.[59]

> On the Holy and Great Thursday, the footwashing ought to be done by the very reverend superior in the narthex of the church, where there is also an icon of the footwashing of the Savior, according to the ordo contained in the Synaxary and the form therein.[60]

The author of the typikon took for granted that a footwashing would be celebrated—indeed the ritual to be followed was already contained in the Synaxary. The main purpose of this passage was not to authorize the footwashing ceremony, but merely to specify where it would take place. The choice of the narthex has nothing to do with the fact that these were women, for male footwashings were often held there as well. What is important about the location is the presence of the icon, which depicted Jesus' own washing of his disciples' feet. This permits us no doubt about what kind of rite these nuns were celebrating. Their footwashing was not a historical fluke, a bizarre custom that only accidentally resembled the "real" footwashings of the men, an anachronistic oddity like the mitred deaconesses of north Africa.[61] The icon that overlooked

[59] *The Alexiad of Anna Comnena,* trans. R. A. Sewter (Baltimore: Penguin, 1969).

[60] Paul Gautier, "Le typikon de la Théotokos Kécharitôménè," *Revue des Études Byzantines* 43 (1985) 125.

[61] See Gregory Dix, *The Shape of the Liturgy,* 2nd ed. (London: Dacre, 1945; repr. New York: Seabury Press, 1982) 405.

this scene is our guarantee that this superior intended to do, and was acknowledged to be doing, what Jesus did with his disciples and commanded us to do also.

In short the participation of women in footwashing rites is not a modern American innovation, but the authentic liturgical tradition of the Church. It is possible (I know of no historical investigation) that footwashings died out among women religious sometime after the Middle Ages, and may thus have been rare or unheard of in the modern era. But there was never a time prior to our own when women were formally excluded from footwashing rites; their participation was limited only by cultural constraints and by the fact that some footwashings were closed to the laity altogether. The real modern innovation is the exclusion of women, not their inclusion; it is the current Sacramentary, not the unofficial American practice, that departs from tradition. Understanding how this unfortunate situation came about is crucial to understanding the concepts underlying the rite we celebrate now, the true nature of our present predicament, and what will be required to get out of it.

V

The Reform of 1956

After several years of experimentation authorized by Pope Pius XII, the reformed rite of Holy Week was published in 1956.[62] Significant changes from previous practice included the restoration of the Easter vigil and other services to their proper times, and the expansion of opportunities for participation by the laity. As the Sacred Congregation of Rites stated at the time, the reforms sought to correct the "common and universal experience . . . that these liturgical services of the sacred triduum are often performed by the clergy with the body of the church nearly deserted."[63]

A. Principles Underlying the Reform

During the years of experimentation, specialists had disagreed over what to do about the footwashing. One discussion, held at the liturgical congress in Lugano in 1953, followed

[62]*Ordo Hebdomadae Sanctae Instauratus,* editio typica (Vatican City: Typis Polyglottis Vaticanis, 1956).

[63]In the decree *Maxima redemptionis nostrae mysteria,* see *Acta Apostolicae Sedis* 47 (1955) 838–41, especially 839. I am quoting the translation published in Frederick R. McManus, *The Rites of Holy Week: Ceremonies, Preparations, Music, Commentary* (Paterson, N.J.: Saint Anthony Guild Press, 1956) 138.

a paper by the eminent professor Hermann Schmidt, S.J. Schmidt had suggested that the footwashing, with its gospel reading, replace the traditional Liturgy of the Word in the Mass of the day. This would help bring things into line with the gospel chronology: the footwashing would be celebrated during the Mass just as Jesus had originally done it during the Last Supper,[64] in keeping with the principle that the services should be restored to their correct times. Nevertheless some of the other scholars present were unwilling to allow the footwashing to eclipse half of the Mass.

A competing suggestion made about the same time was to revive the *Mandatum Pauperum,* but as a public ceremony with the laity present, one that would inspire the Christian people to make Holy Thursday a day specially devoted to charitable works, or at least to contribute to a special collection for the poor which would be taken up while the feet were being washed.[65] There were also those who felt that washing feet

---

[64]The paper Schmidt read at the Lugano Congress, with a transcript of the discussion that followed, were published as "Spirito e storia del giovedì santo" in *Partecipazione attiva alla liturgia: Atti del III convegno internazionale di studi liturgici, Lugano, 14–18 settembre 1943,* eds. Luigi Agustoni and Giovanni Wagner, Collana Liturgica 1 (Lugano: Centro di liturgia e pastorale; Como: Ars Comacina, 1953) 133–56, 163–66. A French text was published in *La Maison-Dieu* 37 (1954) 66–92 and a German text in *Liturgisches Jahrbuch* 3 (1953) 234–52, 260–62.

[65]See, for instance, J. Löw, C.SS.R., "La réforme liturgique du Triduum Sacrum," *Les Questions Liturgiques et Paroissiales* 35 (1954) 9–21, especially 12. This approach was still being advocated after the reformed rite had been published, by A. Bugnini, C. M., and C. Braga, C. M., *Ordo Hebdomadae Sanctae Instauratus: Commentarium ad S.R.C. decretum "Maxima redemptionis nostrae mysteria" diei 16 Novembris 1955 et ad "Ordinem Hebdomadae Sanctae Instauratum,"* Bibliotheca "Ephemerides Liturgicae" Sectio Historica 25 (Rome: Edizioni Liturgiche, 1956) 74, 89. The relevant passages could be translated: "To give this rite meaning again, in recent years, it has been changed into so-called 'paraliturgical actions,' either as a catechetical activity, or as an act of charity among different groups of the faithful. There were also those who sought to have this rite introduced into the liturgy of Holy Thursday, in the didactic part of the Mass, even before

was so inherently foreign to modern culture that it could not possibly serve any meaningful purpose in modern worship, and should thus simply be dropped.

The rite that resulted was a compromise. A new option permitted the footwashing to be inserted into the Mass of the day ("where pastoral reasons recommend this," the rubrics said), but did not require it. If it was not done during the Mass, there was no provision for celebrating it separately at any other time. The Liturgy of the Word was however retained, with the footwashing placed after the gospel (and the homily), which would now have to be read only once. The Mass itself was moved to the evening, replacing Vespers, and thus to about the time the footwashing had always been celebrated. The task of washing the feet thus fell to the celebrant of the Mass, but instead of washing the feet of the other clergy or of poor people he was now to wash the feet of twelve men ("viri"). This enabled some of the laity to be involved, and it was the first time in history that a footwashing was officially restricted to males.

> In the center of the sanctuary, or in the body of the church, benches are prepared on each side for the twelve men ["viri"] whose feet are to be washed. . . .
> Meanwhile the deacon and subdeacon lead the twelve men who have been selected, two by two, to the places prepared, and the choir or the assisting clergy begin the antiphons . . . . The twelve men make a reverence to the altar and to the celebrant, who remains seated in the sanctuary. They then take

the chanting of the Gospel. The Restored Order of Holy Week introduces this rite back into the liturgy, though with permission to celebrate it only where pastoral reasons recommend this, in other words when it can effectively move [the people] to works of Christian charity. . . . It is fitting, where possible, that paupers be selected from among the more indigent of the parish. During the rite let there be a collection taken up among the faithful, so that alms may be given to the paupers whose feet are washed. Finally the faithful should be exhorted to abound in works of charity and mercy throughout the course of Holy Thursday, so that this day may be a 'day of charity.' "

their seats and the sacred ministers go to the celebrant. All
remove their maniples, and the celebrant removes his chasuble as well. . . . Meanwhile the celebrant proceeds to the
washing of the feet. . . .[66]

Why was it decided that the twelve whose feet were washed
had to be males? No doubt this was partly a vestige of the
recent practice in which only male clergy or male paupers were
used, except perhaps within some women's religious houses.
Those who drew up the new rite would not have felt free to
open it to women in any event, at a time when women were
still officially forbidden even to sing in liturgical choirs. But
there was an even more troubling reason than any of these.
Underlying the 1956 reform there was a basic scepticism about
the rite itself, and thus a deliberate (though, of course, well-
intentioned) attempt was made to break with tradition, turn-
ing the ceremony into something quite new. The story was
told by Schmidt himself in his detailed and erudite commentary on the Holy Week reforms.[67]

It was during the liturgical congress at Lugano in 1953 that
we proposed, not without opposition, putting the footwashing after the chanting of the Gospel at Mass. In the reformed
rite of Holy Week this was done as an option.

It is a new evolution in the history of the Mandatum. In
the modern social order the Mandatum Pauperum would have
to be considered unsuitable, particularly because it would for-
cibly humiliate the poor people [involved]. Besides that the
public washing of feet no longer has a place among the customs of modern civilization. For that reason the Mandatum
was made into an appropriate ceremony which illustrates the
words of the Gospel in a theatrical manner. In other words,
in the reformed rite of Holy Week the Mandatum is a symbolic liturgical drama. Because of changed circumstances the

[66]I am using the translation published in McManus, *Rites of Holy Week,*
74–75.
[67]H. Schmidt, S.J., ed., *Hebdomada Sancta,* 2 vols. (Rome: Herder,
1956–1957).

possibility was created that the Mandatum Fratrum could be changed from a secular supper into the Lord's Supper (i.e. the Eucharist). Therefore, so that it might be celebrated worthily, honorably, and devoutly, a ritual, symbolic, liturgical performance is necessary, one that is devoid of secular character. For that reason let twelve honorable brothers be selected, let them be dressed in liturgical vestments, let them walk in procession wearing sandals, etc., etc.[68]

In short, the shape the footwashing took in 1956 was the result of several interacting compromises. The suggestion to insert the footwashing into the Mass was accepted, but the Liturgy of the Word was kept also, and the footwashing thus became a kind of extension of the sermon by way of acting out the gospel story. Those who disapproved of this innovation, or opposed a footwashing rite altogether, had the option of leaving it out. Those who favored a restored *Mandatum Pauperum* got only part of what they wanted. The rubric calling for "viri" did not require that the men be identifiably poor, but pastors who wanted to use poor men were not forbidden to do so. The Instruction of the Sacred Congregation of Rites endorsed one idea that proponents of the *Mandatum Pauperum* considered important: "the faithful are to be taught . . . to be generous in the works of Christian charity on this day."[69] But nothing was said about this in the actual liturgical rubrics. The result of all these compromises was that the footwashing was transformed into something it had never been before. Instead of expressing the unity in love that binds a worshipping community together and reaches beyond even to outsiders and the poor, the footwashing now became a "symbolic liturgical drama" to be watched. The priest now "played" the "role" of Christ, as (since Vatican II) he also does at the reading of the Passions. The twelve males, of course, "played" the apostles, so that there had to be twelve and they had to be male. Pastors who studied the Instruction

[68]Trans. from Schmidt, *Hebdomada Sancta* vol. 2, 775–76.
[69]McManus, *Rites of Holy Week,* 142.

issued by the Sacred Congregation of Rites would have known
that the purpose of the ceremony was "to manifest the Lord's
commandment of brotherly love," and that "the faithful are
to be taught the profound significance of this sacred rite."
But this was conceived in very individualistic terms, as encouraging each member of the congregation "to be generous
in the works of Christian charity."[70] This was, after all, still
the pre-Conciliar Latin liturgy; no one seems to have real-
ized that the rite could have been a communal act, which
would not only manifest, but actually help to effect, the
strengthening of brotherly love within the parish. Thus it was
not designed to achieve this end.

But these compromises are not the only weaknesses in the
footwashing rite of 1956. Each of the positions that contributed
to the compromise raises its own cluster of difficult questions,
many of which seem never to have been debated fully. But
now that the ceremony that resulted from the compromise
has begun to cause severe pastoral problems, this debate is
long overdue.

B. Issues Raised by the Reform

1. Footwashing and Modern Culture

First, those who felt that footwashing rites are incongru-
ous with modern culture were a minority even in the Europe
of 1956; their view is still harder to defend in the worldwide
Church of today, with its endless variety of cultures and customs. It is not clear to what degree the washing of feet was
a familiar custom in Jesus' own time,[71] but his action must

[70]Ibid.

[71]Whether or not Jesus and the apostles were familiar with a contemporary custom of washing feet, they presumably did know that such practices are referred to in the Hebrew scriptures. A number of times it is stated
that a host gave water to his guests for the washing of their feet (Genesis
18:4, 19:2, 24:32, 43:24, Judges 19:21), or that travelers would wash their
own feet at the end of a journey (2 Samuel 11:8, Tobit 6:3, Song of Songs

have been extraordinary even in its original context or it would not have been remembered. Certainly his call to love beckons us to do more than what is comfortable, customary, familiar. Nor should liturgical customs be dropped merely because they are antiquated or exotic—else we Americans would have to give up candles, vestments, the common cup, even reading aloud from books now that everything else is on video.

2. Service to the Poor

Second, those who are reluctant to revive the *Mandatum Pauperum* may be too pessimistic. Certainly one would not want to encourage patronizing attitudes toward the poor, or the idea that parading a few of them through an annual ritual absolves an individual or parish of further obligation. Nor would one want to do anything that would make the poor people involved feel embarrassed, but this is not necessarily inevitable. Right now in the United States, when the churches are increasingly involved in attempts to remedy the injustices of our society, it is by no means uncommon to see members of the homeless and other deprived groups willingly identifying themselves to dramatize their plight publicly. A renewed *Mandatum Pauperum* could perhaps make a powerful statement to our imperfect society that we follow One who said "When you did this for the least of my brethren, you did it to me" (Matthew 25:40), though of course it should not be permitted to deteriorate into a merely political "demonstration." Alert pastors may find other possibilities too. In the centers of our largest cities, for instance, there are parishes that minister during the week to business people who commute in from

5:3). But it is often unclear whether the washing itself was done by the host, the host's servants, or the guests themselves (see also Job 29:6). On the other hand, when King David's servants came to Abigail with an offer of royal marriage, she prostrated herself and replied, "Consider your servant a slave to wash the feet of my lord's servants"—but then quickly mounted a donkey and rode off to marry David (1 Samuel 25:40-42)!

the suburbs, but that celebrate the Lord's Day only with the elderly and impoverished who actually live in the neighborhood. Could a sensitively handled footwashing rite help these two groups move toward becoming a united Christian community?

3. Liturgical Drama

Third, the idea of the footwashing as a kind of liturgical drama opens a particularly thorny morass of issues. Of course many parts of the liturgy recall things Jesus did, and does eternally. But when, if ever, is it appropriate for such a recollection to become a theatrical reenactment? In particular, can a liturgical play be appropriate right in the middle of a Eucharistic celebration?

It is true that the medieval liturgy included dramas at certain points, on certain days, but they differed greatly from each other in many respects, including the degree to which and the manner in which they were attached to the liturgy, as well as the extent to which they made use of non-liturgical theatrical elements (e.g., costumes, scenery, etc.).[72] Indeed, it is often quite difficult to say exactly where the line should be drawn between liturgical anamnesis and dramatic reenactment. If the person washing the feet wraps himself in a linen towel, this action has an obvious practical purpose, at the same time that it recalls something Jesus himself did. But the towel can easily become a costume, inviting the use of additional costuming. The vessels for holding and pouring the water are obviously indispensable, yet they readily

[72]The classic study of liturgical drama in the medieval Western liturgy is Karl Young, *The Drama of the Medieval Church,* 2 vols. (Oxford: Clarendon Press, 1933). For briefer surveys that also cover the music, see W. L. Smoldon, "Liturgical Drama," *Early Medieval Music Up to 1300,* ed. Dom Anselm Hughes, New Oxford History of Music 2 (London and New York: Oxford University Press, 1954) 175–219. Susan Rankin, "Liturgical Drama," *The Early Middle Ages to 1300,* eds. Richard Crocker and David Hiley, New Oxford History of Music 2, rev. ed. (Oxford and New York: Oxford University Press, 1990) 310–56, and the bibliography, 751–77.

become props, encouraging the addition of further stage paraphernalia. At what point, then, does liturgy cross the line to become drama? And at what point should we judge that the transition has gone too far? Clearly, any serious attempt to reintroduce dramas into the modern liturgy should be informed by a much more thorough and theologically informed investigation of their history than has yet been attempted.[73]

It is in the Byzantine rite, rather than in the West, that the traditional footwashing ceremonies incorporated the greatest number of dramatic elements. This is partly because the footwashing took place during the actual reading from the gospel, instead of being accompanied by chants as in the West. It thus became a kind of "acting out" simultaneous with the reading. Each action was timed to occur just when it was narrated by the reader, so that the line "he began to wash their feet" was repeated eleven times, as the washer began anew with each of the first eleven persons representing the apostles. The twelfth person, as the washer approached, would ask Peter's question, "Lord, are you going to wash my feet?" and he and the washer would repeat the entire dialogue between Jesus and Peter. This tended to lead to further identification of the participants with biblical characters: when the washer repeated Jesus' words "You too are clean, though not all of you are," for example, he would point to the person representing Judas (cf. John 13:10-11). Other gospel passages introduced into the ceremony permitted speaking parts for other apostles, and the reader was at times identified with John the Evangelist.[74]

[73]I particularly recommend the two following articles by Margot Fassler: *"Danielis ludus* and the Feast of Fools: Popular Tradition in a Thirteenth-Century Cathedral Play," *Plainsong in the Age of Polyphony,* ed. Thomas Forrest Kelly, Cambridge Studies in Performance Practice 2 (Cambridge University Press, 1992) 65-99. "The Representation of Time in the *Ordo representacionis ade,"* *Contexts: Style and Values in Medieval Art and Literature,* Yale French Studies: Special Issue, eds. Daniel Poirion and Nancy Freeman Regalado (New Haven: Yale University Press, 1991) 97-113.

[74]See Pétridès, "Le lavement" and "La cérémonie."

As this ceremony was carried out in recent times by the Greek patriarch of Jerusalem, it may be judged to have stayed within the bounds of liturgical worship. In the case of the foot-washing celebrated on the island of Patmos, however, one may judge that the line has been crossed, and the ceremony moved from liturgy to theater.

The stage at Patmos is not placed before the monastery or the church, but in the middle of the public square. It is decorated with flowers, candles, crosses and liturgical fans. In the middle of the stage is placed a chair where the superior will sit for the washing; in front of this chair is a low table, to the right and left are seats for the apostles. One goes up to this makeshift scene by a wooden stairway built on one side. In one corner of the square, far from the stage, an icon of the Savior is placed. Taking part in the festivity are eleven monks of the holy Monastery and one layman, destined to play the role of Judas; he is payed thirty florins, always according to the gospel text [i.e. Matthew 26:15]. To this is added a pair of boots at the end of the performance, and the whole crowd despises this poor wretch, forced by his extreme poverty to accept the role of traitor, and destined during all his life to be hated by his compatriots. Thus the one who plays this role is usually an unknown from some other village, for the Patmos performance of the Washing attracts a huge crowd from all over Greece to attend this spectacle.

At the appointed time, usually two in the afternoon (to give the public a chance to attend the evening office of Holy Thursday), the monks who will take part come, two by two, down the hill from the monastery to the square, dressed in purple velvet, clerical hats covered by veils, with pomp and magnificence and in the following order: Andrew and James of Alphaeus, Simon and Thaddeus, Matthew and Bartholomew, Philip and Thomas, James and John of Zebedee, and finally Peter and Judas. The superior walks beside the reader of the gospel. Four deacons come afterward carrying censers, with which they incense the public as they pass; they are followed by a great number of chanters.

Having arrived at the square, after a short prayer pronounced by the superior, they proceed to the Washing, accompanied by the reading of three gospels (Mark 10:32-34, Matthew 20:22-29, and John 13:1-11). During the reading, the superior mimes the Washing as well as all the other details contained in the text. But when a dialogue occurs in the readings, it really takes place between the personages involved, particularly between Peter and the Lord, following the Gospel tradition. After that the superior exchanges his monastic habit for priestly vestments, this time preparing himself for a more grandiose scene. He hears the reading of a fourth gospel (John 13:12-18), after which, following a new solemn prayer, he proceeds to the scene of Jesus on the Mount of Olives. It is the most theatrical part of the play, for it is no longer interrupted by any reading.[75]

After re-enacting the scene of the Agony in the Garden, the monks process back to the monastery, accompanied by the singing of a famous hymn, composed in the ninth century by Kassia the nun:

The woman who had fallen into many sins, perceiving Thy divinity, O Lord, fulfilled the part of a myrrh-bearer; and with lamentations she brought sweet-smelling oil of myrrh to Thee before Thy burial. "Woe is me," she said, "for night surrounds me, dark and moonless, and stings my lustful passion with the love of sin. Accept the fountain of my tears, O Thou who drawest down from the clouds the waters of the sea. Incline to the groanings of my heart, O Thou who in

[75]Translated from the French summary given in Vénétia Cottas, *Le Théatre à Byzance* (Paris: Librairie Orientaliste Paul Geuthner, 1931) 128–30. Cottas in turn was following the desciption in A. A. Dmitrievsky, *Patmoskie otcherki* (Kiev, 1894) 236, which seems to be unavailable in North America. Cottas identifies the third gospel reading as John 14:1-11, but this is surely an error for John 13:1-11. It is not clear what is to be made of Cottas' statement that the superior "mimes" during the reading (she uses the French word "mime"). I doubt it was intended to mean (as it would in English) that he silently acts out the washing without using actual water or other props.

Thine ineffable self-emptying hast bowed down the heavens.
I shall kiss Thy most pure feet and wipe them with the hairs
of my head, those feet whose sound Eve heard at dusk in Para-
dise, and hid herself for fear. Who can search out the multi-
tude of my sins and the abyss of Thy judgements, O Savior
of my soul? Despise me not, Thine handmaiden, for Thou
hast mercy without measure.''[76]

The Patmos footwashing retains many liturgical elements—
the processions, the deacons with censers, the choir, the icon,
the prayers, the readings. It preserves aspects of both the *Mandatum Fratrum* (in the eleven monks and their superior) and
the *Mandatum Pauperum* (in the pauper who plays Judas). But
there are also some theatrical elements: the action takes place
on a stage rather than in church, and each participant is identified with a specific biblical character, even though only a
few actually have ''lines'' or actions assigned to them in the
scriptural text. In fact the theatricality is relatively restrained
—there are no costumes or scenery, for instance. Nevertheless, with the introduction of other material leading up to the
betrayal of Jesus by Judas, the logic of the theater has begun
to obscure what would have been important themes of a purely
liturgical ceremony. The emphasis on re-enactment is so
strong that the superior seems more to be playing the historical Jesus than to be deliberately imitating Jesus' example of
humility. Most seriously, the treatment of the one pauper directly contradicts the authentic spirit of the footwashing:
Though he is given money and a pair of boots, he is made
to play the villain's role of Judas—even the money he receives
is the same amount that Judas was paid to betray Jesus. As

[76]Mother Mary and Kallistos Ware, *The Lenten Triodion,* 540-41. For
further discussions of the text and melody, see Jørgen Raasted, ''Voice
and Verse in a Troparion of Cassia,'' *Studies in Eastern Chant* 3 (London:
Oxford University Press, 1973) 171-78. Diane Touliatos-Banker, ''Women
Composers of Medieval Byzantine Chant,'' *College Music Symposium* 24/1
(1984) 62-80, especially 76-80.

a result he is so despised by the audience that only a very poor person who is unknown locally can be found to accept the part.

In any case, the Western liturgical tradition never developed anything like the Patmos play. Indeed the German Abbess Herrad of Hohenburg (1167–1195) chose the footwashing to illustrate the difference between the devoutness appropriate to the liturgy and the buffoonery that accompanied the liturgical dramas of her time.[77] Thus the footwashing rite produced by the 1956 reform of Holy Week was not in any sense a return to tradition, but rather an attempt to create something new, a liturgical play that had never been part of the liturgy before. It was not a revival of earlier Western practices, and it owed nothing to the rites of the East.

It is not surprising, then, that the 1956 transformation of the footwashing into a re-enactment changes the entire dynamic of this rite as it relates to the prayer of the whole Christian people. For example, because the celebrant now takes the role of Christ, the most important characteristic of the *Mandatum Fratrum* is lost whenever this priest is not the usual leader of the community. (This will always be the case, for instance, in religious communities of women.) In the liturgical tradition it was always the community's own superior who taught Christ's example by following it herself or himself, the head and teacher of all becoming the servant of all. Where there is no such reversal, because the celebrating priest is not the head of the community, the entire ceremony can never be more than a show, for the main liturgical sign is missing.

Moreover, even if it is right that the footwashing should be a theatrical re-enactment, this would not justify the requirement that biological males represent the apostles—or even Jesus himself. Throughout the worldwide history of drama, even Christian liturgical drama,[78] there have always been ac-

---

[77]See Young, *The Drama,* vol. 1, 98–99; vol. 2, 412–14.

[78]For instance in the earliest and most important liturgical drama, the *Visitatio Sepulchri* celebrated on Easter morning, the three women who came to anoint Jesus' body in the tomb were typically "played" by male monks

cepted conventions permitting actors of one gender to play characters belonging to the other, without necessarily conveying any suggestion of lewdness. If the play is the thing, even a "symbolic ritual" play, then acting ability more than biological gender should determine who gets the part.

or canons. See Young, *Drama,* vol. 1, 201–450, and especially the frontispiece, a medieval depiction of monks acting in this play, vested in albs, chasubles, and wimples. For new information on the origins of this drama see my forthcoming article "The Oriental Background of the Easter Sepulchre Play."

VI

The Footwashing Since Vatican II

The new footwashing rite of 1956 was simplified after Vatican II, but essentially left unchanged. The word "viri" was unfortunately kept, though the requirement that there be twelve of them was dropped. Thus it is a novelty, with all its questionable departures from tradition, that is the obligatory basis of our present liturgical practice. The heated battles over the word "viri" are actually not about fidelity to tradition, but about fidelity to an innovation, indeed to a mistake. It is instructive, however, to compare the present Roman usage with the reformed Ambrosian rite, which integrates more successfully the insights of Vatican II with the actual liturgical tradition, and which demonstrates that a rite need not insist on "viri" to be approved by the Vatican. The Ambrosian rite, now celebrated only in the diocese of Milan, was not subject to the 1956 Holy Week reforms of the Roman rite—nevertheless it anticipated one of them by more than a century. In 1840, the *Mandatum Pauperum* was moved from the archbishop's apartments to the Duomo, so that what had been a private affair became a public celebration. On Holy Thursday evening, in the presence of the canons, the archbishop washed the right feet of twelve elderly men from a local hospice, and gave them purses of money, eleven white and one purple, representing the fact that one of the apostles

betrayed Jesus.[79] After Vatican II, the option to follow the
new Roman practice by inserting the footwashing into the
Mass was rejected, though it was permitted to wash feet immediately before or after the Mass. But instead of twelve paupers, the rubrics now call only for twelve of the "faithful
[fideles]"; the word "viri" appears nowhere. Whether or not
women actually take part in the footwashings in Milan, therefore, at least there is no rubrical basis for excluding them.[80]
   The differences between the modern Ambrosian and
Roman rites show how arbitrary and even capricious the
Roman rite actually is. It didn't have to be this way, and it
still doesn't. Yet the fact that it remains the only authorized
rite for nearly all Western rite Catholics raises disturbing questions about the way liturgical renewal is now being carried
out in the Roman communion: A small number of scholars,
uncertain how to renew a tradition that in some sense goes
back to the earliest period of the Church, indeed to a command of Jesus himself, compromised by changing it into something it had never been before, thereby imposing a novelty
on almost the entire Western Church. A generation later, despite yet another liturgical reform, the new rite has begun to
cause pastoral difficulties the innovators could not possibly
have foreseen—yet the innovations that are causing the problems are no longer recognized as such, for both sides assume
that they represent hoary tradition. Worst of all, there is no
mechanism in place for changing them. As a result the problem festers on and on, emerging each year during the holiest

---

[79]*Messale Ambrosiano* (Milan: Pia Società S. Paolo, 1949) 478–79.

[80]"Si mandatum praecedit vel sequitur missam, sacerdos indutus manet
paramentis missae; alias pluviale violacei coloris induit. Nunquam mandatum fieri potest infra missam. Sacerdos procedit ad locum ubi sedent
duodecim fideles, pede dextro detecto. Deposito pro opportunitate pluviali
vel casula, sacerdos accedit ad locum lotionis; genuflexus singulis lavat
pedem dextrum et abstersum osculatur." *Missale Ambrosianum iuxta ritum
Sanctae Ecclesiae Mediolanensis ex Decreto Sacrosancti Œcumenici Concilii Vaticani
II Instauratum . . .* (Milan: Centro Ambrosiano di Documentazione e di
Studi Religiosi, 1981) 229–30.

period to sting, yet again, many people who already feel alienated from the Church. It is hard to imagine anything more opposed to the teaching of Vatican II that the liturgy is an act of the whole people of God.[81]

The right of the whole Christian people to participate actively in the Church's worship should not mean merely that they may watch while a select few of their number get to carry out minor tasks in the sanctuary, or even sing or have the texts in front of them during the proceedings. More important is their right to be taught and nourished by the complete and authentic liturgical tradition, "in the living communion which exists between us and our brothers who are in the glory of heaven."[82] For the liturgical tradition is a vast treasury of rites, hymns, and prayers from many periods and languages—yet the bulk of this treasure is known only to specialist scholars. The great majority of Christians, including most of the clergy, have no access to it at all except through the worship that is actually carried out in our modern churches. This is why it is extremely important that those who are responsible for renewal and reform of the rites take care to preserve as much as possible, not only of what is judged to be their authentic spirit, but even of their historic content. No individual or group is smart enough—or should be powerful enough—to replace the legitimate tradition with (even well-meant) private fancy, and indeed the Council forbade this very thing.[83] The problems that have emerged in the footwashing service demonstrate what frightful dislocations can result when the liturgical tradition is arbitrarily compromised.

---

[81]See the Dogmatic Constitution on the Church *(Lumen gentium)* arts. 10-11. A convenient English translation is in *Vatican Council II: The Conciliar and Post Conciliar Documents,* ed. Austin Flannery, new rev. ed. (Collegeville, Minnesota: The Liturgical Press, 1984) 360-63.

[82]Dogmatic Constitution on the Church *(Lumen gentium)* art. 51; see *Vatican Council II,* 412-13.

[83]Constitution on the Sacred Liturgy *(Sacrosanctum Concilium)* arts. 22-23. See *Vatican Council II,* 9-10.

Similarly, the active participation of the whole Church in the liturgy will never be fully achieved without active participation in the very processes of renewal, revision, and reform. The broad international dialogue among all scholarly researchers, the practical experience of pastors throughout the world, and the consensus of the whole faithful—each is a forum whose judgment, though not final, is indispensable. A way must be found to ensure that all these voices are heard in the ongoing liturgical renewal, while still permitting decisions and approvals to be made in an orderly and speedy manner. Creating such a broad consultative process could hardly be easy, particularly when we have lived through decades of liturgical chaos already. But the footwashing issue amply demonstrates that the alternative (i.e., the situation we have now) is even worse.

Given circumstances as they are, then, what should be done? At the very least, it should be officially decided that the word "viri" in the Sacramentary may be ignored, or (better) changed to "fideles," as in the Ambrosian rite. However, it is clear by now that the offending word is not the whole of the problem, but only a symptom of a much more basic difficulty in the rite itself. It would be best if this rite could be discarded altogether, as a failed experiment or a historical aberration, and replaced with something more representative of the fullness of tradition. But it is easy to tear down, difficult to build up: What should a more authentic, renewed footwashing rite actually look like? Appended to this essay is my own suggestion for such a rite. Drawn up by one who is a historian, rather than a theologian or pastor, it is intended only to illustrate some of the ways that modern American worshippers could avail themselves more fully of the complete liturgical tradition. Each worshipping community will need to reflect on its own history, pastoral situation, and denominational traditions to determine how helpful to its own liturgical life my suggestions may be.

Even under the best of circumstances (and who was ever lucky enough to live then?), the revision of a rite takes time.

Until a renewed rite can be drawn up and made officially available for use, what should be done? In places where the participation of women in the footwashing has not been treated as controversial, it may be possible to carry on much as before. But given the intractability of human nature, there will probably still be those who feel they must remain faithful to the word "viri." It would probably be best if diocesan or parish policies that exclude women could simply be banned altogether at the national level, on the grounds that they violate the present national policy that "with the exception of service at the altar itself, women may be admitted to the exercise of other liturgical ministries."[84] In the more difficult parish situations, the best solution for the time being may be to make greater use of the rubric permitting the footwashing to be omitted entirely, while at the same time using the homily to convey a sound understanding of Jesus' actions and his command to us. Some groups may be able to hold their own footwashings, provided this is not done in a spirit of anger or divisiveness that would contradict the basic meaning of the ceremony —"for God is a God not of disorder but of peace" (1 Corinthians 14:33). Communities that follow the Benedictine Rule, for instance, already have a clear mandate to celebrate footwashings on their own.

[84]This policy, adopted by the Bishop's Committee on the Liturgy in February 1971, is stated in the "Appendix to the General Instruction for the Dioceses of the United States of America," par. 66, in the front of the Sacramentary; see *The Sacramentary*, 47. The statement is also published, with a brief essay on its historical background, in Frederick R. McManus, ed. *Thirty Years of Liturgical Renewal: Statements of the Bishops' Committee on the Liturgy* (Washington, D.C.: Secretariat, Bishops' Committee on the Liturgy, 1987) 134–37.

VII

Toward a Renewed Rite for the Washing of Feet

A. Introduction

In view of the present confusion, the rubrics of a renewed rite should begin with an explanation of what the ceremony means. As always, I advocate staying as close as possible to the scriptural, patristic, and liturgical sources. Section 1 of the suggested rite is my attempt to do this. Next, the rubrics of the new rite ought to define clearly who should participate. The suggestion in section 2 seeks to preserve the best features of both the *Mandatum Fratrum* and the *Mandatum Pauperum,* emphasizing both the buildling up of love within the community and its reaching outward to others. Paragraph 3 attempts to restore the tradition that the highest-ranking person in the community should be the one to wash the feet of the others. This is logically the celebrant if the footwashing takes place during Mass in a parish church, but in houses of religious it ought to be the superior. In more informal groupings, it is best for the washing to be done by "the person or persons who usually lead the community," while groups that have no recognized leader are probably small enough and cohesive enough to work out their own arrangements.

Paragraph 4 seeks to restore the possibility of celebrating the footwashing in connection with a community meal, or as an independent service outside of Mass. This should benefit communities that, for whatever reason, cannot necessarily share the same Eucharist, or that have adopted patterns of leadership that may be incompatible with the present all-male priesthood.

Paragraph 5 follows the broad outlines of the traditional Western order of service: gospel reading (perhaps with a homily or brief explanation, though this is not traditional), washing accompanied by singing, closing prayer. The three Gregorian antiphons used here were selected from the large repertory of traditional material. Though our present Sacramentary gives pride of place to texts that retell the gospel story of the footwashing, the preference here has been for texts that explain the meaning of the rite. Thus our suggested rite restores to first place the traditional opening antiphon *Mandatum novum,* ''A new commandment I give you.'' Two other similar antiphons with psalms follow.[85] Instead of or in addition to these, it is also possible to sing *Ubi caritas*[86] or another appropriate hymn. The decision as to which texts will actually be sung in a particular celebration will of course be made by the ministers of music.

For the concluding prayer, several options are offered. The first is derived from the nineteenth-century Gallican-inspired collect *Deus totius caritatis,* eliminating the part about Mary Magdalene. The second option is an English rendering of the traditional collect *Adesto Domine* of the Roman Missal. The third prayer is *Respice Domine,* taken from the Romano-Germanic Pontifical of the tenth century, and the fourth is from the Byzantine-rite footwashing used by the Greek patriarch of Jerusalem.[87]

---

[85]For their sources, see fn. 42 and 45.

[86]For sources and translations, see fn. 46.

[87]For the sources, see fn. 51–54 above.

B. The Mandatum: A Rite for the Washing of Feet

1. The Meaning of the Footwashing Rite

The Lord Jesus, knowing that he was about to be humiliated in death, washed the feet of his disciples, and commanded them to wash each other's feet. He did this as a sign of the heritage of eternal life that he meant to share with them, and as an example of humility that he wanted them to imitate. In doing this he revealed "his ineffable love for them . . . as 'His own.' "[88]—a love so self-abasing that it reached out "not only to those for whom he was about to endure death, but even to the one who was about to betray him to death."[89]

The Church washes feet today in obedience to the mandate of Jesus to "wash each other's feet" (John 13:14), and to teach the virtue of humility. For the humility of Christ is ultimately the mystery of the incarnation: "God was made man for us, as an example of humility and to manifest God's love for us. For it profits us to believe, and to keep firmly and unshakenly in our heart, that the humility, whereby God was born of a woman and was led through such great insults to His death by mortal men, is the most excellent medicine by which the swelling of our pride may be cured, and the exalted mystery by which the chain of sin may be broken."[90] Thus the humility that ought to be practiced by Christians is more than a merely penitential or virtuous act—it is through

[88]St. John Chrysostom, *Patrologia Graeca,* ed. J.-P. Migne (Paris: J.-P. Migne, 1857–1866) vol. 59, cols. 381–86, quoting John 13:1. I have quoted the English translation by Sister Thomas Aquinas Goggin, S.C.H.: Saint John Chrysostom, *Commentary on Saint John the Apostle and Evangelist, Homilies 48–88,* The Fathers of the Church: A New Translation (New York: Fathers of the Church, 1960) 254.

[89]St. Augustine, *Tractatus in Johannem* 55:7, edited in Corpus Christianorum, Series Latina (Vienna, 1866–) vol. 36, 466.

[90]St. Augustine, *De Trinitate* 8:5, edited in Corpus Christianorum, Series Latina (Turnhout: Brepols, 1953–) vol. 50, 276. I am using the translation of Stephen McKenna, C.SS.R.: Saint Augustine, *The Trinity* (Washington D.C.: Catholic University of America Press, 1963) 252.

humility that each Christian "will arrive at that 'perfect love' of God 'which casts out fear.' "[91] And it is the humble exercise of love that binds Christians together in the unity for which Christ prayed, a unity that resembles the love between the Father and the Son (John 17:20-26).

The role of humility and love in building up the Christian community is intimately linked to the Divine Humility of Jesus, according to the teaching of the apostle: "Make my joy complete by being of a single mind, one in love, one in heart and one in mind. Nothing is to be done out of jealousy or vanity; instead, out of humility of mind everyone should give preference to others. . . . Make your own the mind of Christ Jesus, who, being in the form of God, did not count equality with God something to be grasped, but emptied himself, taking the form of a slave" (Philippians 2:2-7). The liturgical footwashing is an effective sign of this, "for when the body is bent down at the feet of a brother, the feeling of this humility is also awakened in the heart itself, or strengthened if it was already there."[92]

2. Those Whose Feet May Be Washed

If the community celebrating the footwashing is small or especially intimate, the feet of everyone should be washed. If, however, there are too many people to permit this, a representative number of the faithful may be chosen. Three, twelve (representing the apostles), and thirteen (representing Jesus and the apostles) are traditional numbers, but any number may be used. If the community is especially diverse or has suffered divisions, it may be appropriate to include, as equals, representatives from each of the groups or factions, but only if this will not divert attention from the central fo-

[91]Benedictine Rule 7:67, quoting 1 John 4:18. In the translation *RB 1980*, see p. 201.

[92]St. Augustine, *Tractatus in Johannem* 58:4, edited in Corpus Christianorum, Series Latina (Turnhout: Brepols, 1953–) vol. 36, 474.

cus of the celebration, which is Jesus' own example. It is especially appropriate if some of the representatives are chosen
from among the community's poorest or humblest members,
or from among those who are marginalized or rejected by society at large, provided this is done in a way that will promote genuine love and respect for them, rather than feelings
of superiority or pity. If the worshipping community includes
people of both sexes, then both men and women should be
included among the representatives whose feet are washed,
unless this would seriously conflict with the social customs or
cultural mores of the country or region or group.

If, for any reason, it appears doubtful that celebrating the
footwashing rite will move those who are present to greater
humility and love for one another, it may be pastorally wisest
not to celebrate it at all. In such a case it would be well to
impart to the faithful an accurate understanding of the meaning of Jesus' actions during a homily following the reading
of the gospel.

3. Those Who Wash the Feet

If the footwashing takes place within the evening Eucharist
or Mass of the Lord's Supper on Holy Thursday, the chief
celebrant should wash the feet, assisted by the other celebrants
and ministers. If the footwashing is celebrated on its own, as
a separate service, the religious superior, or the person or persons who usually lead the community, should wash the feet.
The one who does the washing should have assistants to help
with the ewer, the basin, the towels, and whatever else may
be needed.

4. Environments and Contexts for Footwashing Ceremonies

If the footwashing is celebrated within the evening Eucharist
on Holy Thursday, it should of course take place in or near
the sanctuary where the Eucharist is celebrated. If it is celebrated on a different day, or apart from the Eucharist, it may
be joined to a community meal or to Evening Prayer. In such

cases it may be celebrated in any worthy and dignified place that is large enough to hold all the people who will attend.

5. *The Order of Service*

If the footwashing takes place during the Eucharist, it should come immediately after the gospel (John 13:1-17) and the homily. But if the footwashing is celebrated separately from the Mass, it should begin with this reading, followed perhaps by a brief homily explaining the gospel text and the relationship of Jesus' actions to what is about to be celebrated. After the homily let the washing itself begin.

Everyone whose feet will be washed should be seated in a suitable arrangement. If only certain members of the worshipping assembly will be washed, they should be seated in such a way that they can clearly be seen by all. In imitation of Jesus himself (John 13:4), it is traditional for the one who washes the feet to first wrap a linen towel around himself or herself, and to use this towel to dry the feet. But it is also permissible to have one person wash and another dry. The traditional gesture of kissing the feet of each person after washing and drying them should be used only if it will be seen as an expression of Christian love and will not cause scandal.

During the washing and drying of the feet, the choir or the congregation should sing appropriate music. Ideally, the words should recount in some way the gospel story of Jesus washing the feet of his disciples (John 13:1-20), or quote sayings of Jesus about the new commandment of love, particularly John 13:34. But any text about Christian love and service may be used, especially the medieval Latin hymn *Ubi caritas* or a modern translation of it.

The following three psalms, each with its own antiphon, are adapted from traditional Gregorian chants. The people may repeat the antiphon after each verse is sung by a soloist or the choir. The musical rhythm should follow the natural rhythm of the texts. The melodies may of course be transposed to any pitch, as needed.

Antiphon 1

"Man-dá-tum no-vum do vo-bis, ut di - li - gá - tis ín-vi-

cem, si - cut di - léx- i vos," di - cit Dó -mi - nus.

or Antiphon 2

"A new commandment I give you, that you love one an-oth-er,

just as I have loved you," says the Lord.

Psalm 119:1-8

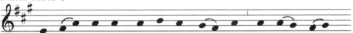

They are hap-py whose life is blame-less, who fol - low

God's law! *Antiphon*

They are hap-py who do his will, seek-ing him with

all their hearts, *Antiphon*

who nev - er do an - y - thing e - vil but walk in

his ways. *Antiphon*

You have laid down your pre-cepts to be o - beyed with

care. *Antiphon*

May my footsteps be firm to o - bey your stat - utes. *Antiphon*

Then I shall not be put to shame as I heed your

com-mands. *Antiphon*

I will thank you with an up-right heart as I learn

your de-crees. *Antiphon*

I will o - bey your stat - utes; do not for-sake me. *Antiphon*

Glo-ry be to the Fa-ther and to the Son and to the

Ho - ly Spir - it *Antiphon*

As it   was in the be-gin-ning, is now, and e-ver shall be,

world without   end.   A-men   *Antiphon*

Antiphon

By this shall they all know that you are my dis-ci - ples

if you have love for   one   an - oth - er.

Psalm 85:8-13

I   will   hear what the Lord God has to say,   a voice that

speaks of peace,   *Antiphon*

peace   for   his peo-ple and his friends, and those who turn

to him in their hearts.   *Antiphon*

His   help   is near for those who fear him   and his glo - ry

will dwell in our land.   *Antiphon*

Mer - cy   and faith-ful-ness have met;   jus-tice and peace

have em - braced.   *Antiphon*

Faith - ful - ness shall spring from the earth and jus-tice look

down from hea - ven.   *Antiphon*

The   Lord   will make us pros-per   and our earth shall

yield its fruit.   *Antiphon*

Jus - tice   shall march before him   and peace shall fol-low

his steps.   *Antiphon*

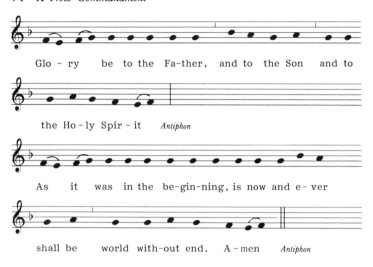

Glo - ry   be to the Fa-ther, and to the Son   and to

the Ho - ly Spir - it   *Antiphon*

As   it   was in the be-gin-ning, is now and e- ver

shall be   world with-out end.   A - men   *Antiphon*

Antiphon

The love of Christ has ga-thered us to - geth - er,

so let us hon-or and love   Christ our God.

Psalm 133

How good and how plea-sant it is,   when bro-thers

[and sis-ters] live in   u - ni - ty!   *Antiphon*

It is   like pre-cious oil up-on the head run-ning

down up - on   the   beard,   *Antiphon*

run - ning   down up-on Aa - ron's   beard,   up-on   the

col-lar   of his   robes.   *Antiphon*

It   is   like   the   dew of Her-mon   which falls on the

heights of Zi - on.   *Antiphon*

For there   the   Lord gives his bless-ing, life for   e - ver.

Glo - ry   be   to the Fa - ther and to the Son,   and   to

the   Ho - ly   Spir - it   *Antiphon*

As   it   was   in the be-gin-ning   is now   and e-ver

shall   be,   world with-out   end. A-men   *Antiphon*

After the feet have been washed, and the vessels and towels placed out of the way, the service may end with one or more of the following prayers, or with a similar prayer:

[From a nineteenth-century Benedictine prayer:]

O God, you strengthen all love and are pleased by it. Your Son bent down in humility toward us, so that we could stand up and be raised to you. As we, your rejoicing family, continue to grow in numbers, grant that we may practice love so actively, that through peace we may remain united in you. We ask this through your Son Jesus, the Savior of the world, who lives and reigns with you in the unity of the Holy Spirit, one God forever and ever.

[The traditional prayer of the Roman Missal:]

Lord Jesus, we ask you to be present as we celebrate our service to each other. Because you willingly washed the feet of your disciples, we ask you to accept what we ourselves do in obedience to your command. Here we wash away outward defilement for each other; may you wash away our inward sins also. For you live and reign with the Father and the Holy Spirit, one God forever and ever.

[A prayer from the tenth century:]

O Lord, look upon these your servants, who have bent down to serve their brothers and sisters, in the dutiful submission of holy obedience. May they always have you for their help, and by their good deeds may they overcome evil. Let nothing prevent them from always being ready to serve, so that they may merit to receive an eternal reward from you. We ask this through Jesus Christ, your Son, who lives and reigns with you and the Holy Spirit, one God, for ever and ever.

[Based on a prayer from the Byzantine Greek rite of Jerusalem:]

O Jesus, Lord our God, in your infinite mercy you emptied yourself and took the form of a slave. At the time of your saving and lifegiving and voluntary Passion, you deigned to have supper with your holy disciples and apostles. After that, wearing a linen towel, you washed the feet of your holy disciples, giving them an example of humility and of mutual love. Then you said, "As I have done for you, you must also do for each other." O Lord, we unworthy servants have followed your example: Come into our midst, remove every spot and defilement from our souls, so that, being washed of the dust that clings to our souls because of our faults, and being wiped dry by the linen towel of your love, we may be made acceptable before you all the days of our lives, and find grace in your presence. For you are the one who blesses and sanctifies all things, O Christ our God. To you we render glory, as to your eternal Father and to your very holy and good and life-giving Spirit, now and always, forever and ever.

Following the prayer, the people may be dismissed in the customary way, unless another celebration is to follow.

VIII
Conclusion

The potential pastoral value of restoring the authentic tradition should not be underestimated. Our modern world, languishing under tyrannies new and old, turns daily to the Church to ask (often in tones of sarcasm and mockery), "Where now is the One who said 'I am among you as one who serves'? Show us a sign of him who taught you 'Love one another as I have loved you'!" What if we, momentarily putting aside questions about tradition, simply tried to formulate the best possible response: What would most effectively show that in the Church—his own people—Jesus eternally humbles himself to take the form of a slave? It is easy to point proudly to what we have already said or done on behalf of the weakest and poorest in our society, as if we expect to be told, "You are not far from the kingdom of God" (Mark 12:34). But in fact we have failed to hear the many voices that are already telling us, "There is still one thing you lack" (Luke 18:22). Among those we have not heard are numerous women, who believe they hear the Church saying to them, "If I do not wash you, you will have no heritage with me." Many of us do not yet realize how many women there are who, reasonably or not, cannot attend any Catholic liturgy without feeling besieged yet again by the myriad cultural messages that deny them their full human dignity, and bind them in a secondary and inferior status. When so many Christian women see the Church as one of the oldest and most powerful accomplices in the oppression of their sex, and are repeatedly hurt and angered by its unyielding insensitivity to their situation, how will the Church speak to them— and to their many non-Christian sympathizers—of the eternal and limitless love that God bends down to extend to us all, and commands us to give to each other? To our world today, mindful of the triumphs and sins of our remembered common past, there could scarcely be a more powerful sign of the humble, utterly self-giving love of Jesus, than a Catholic priest washing the feet of a woman.